A NOISY BOOK!

by ross

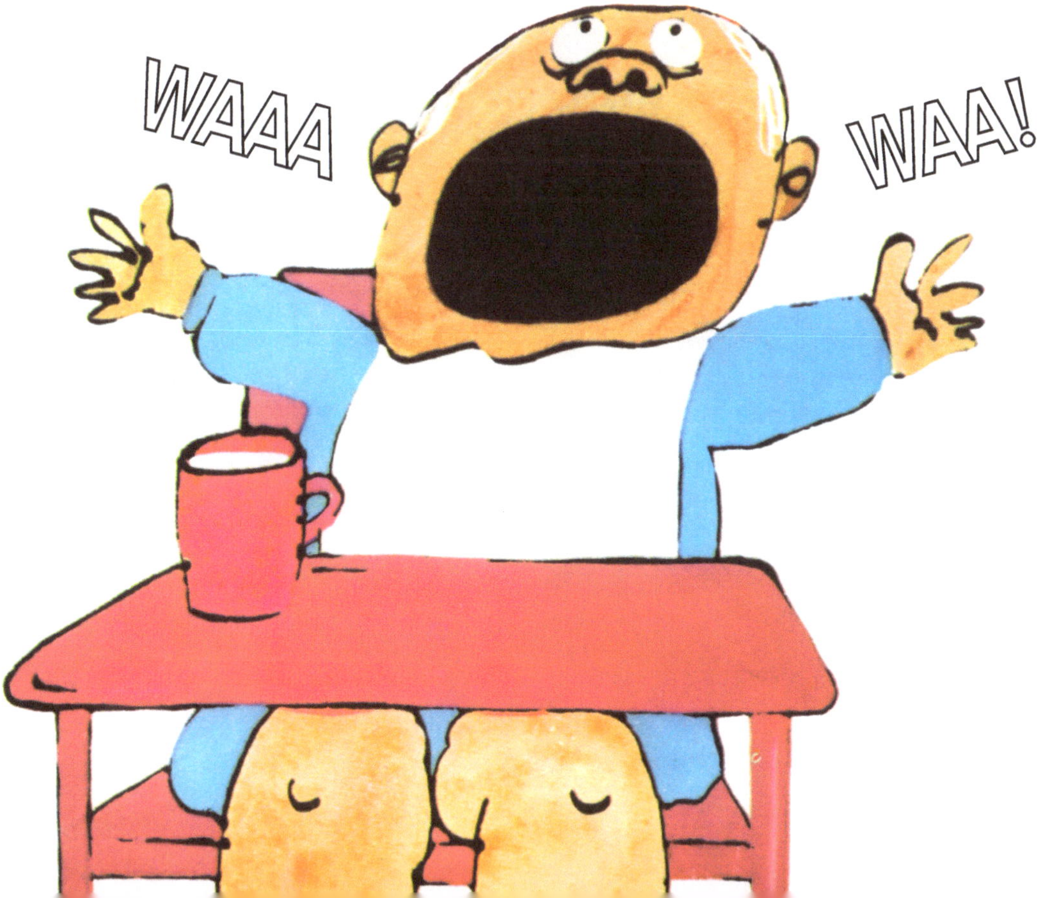

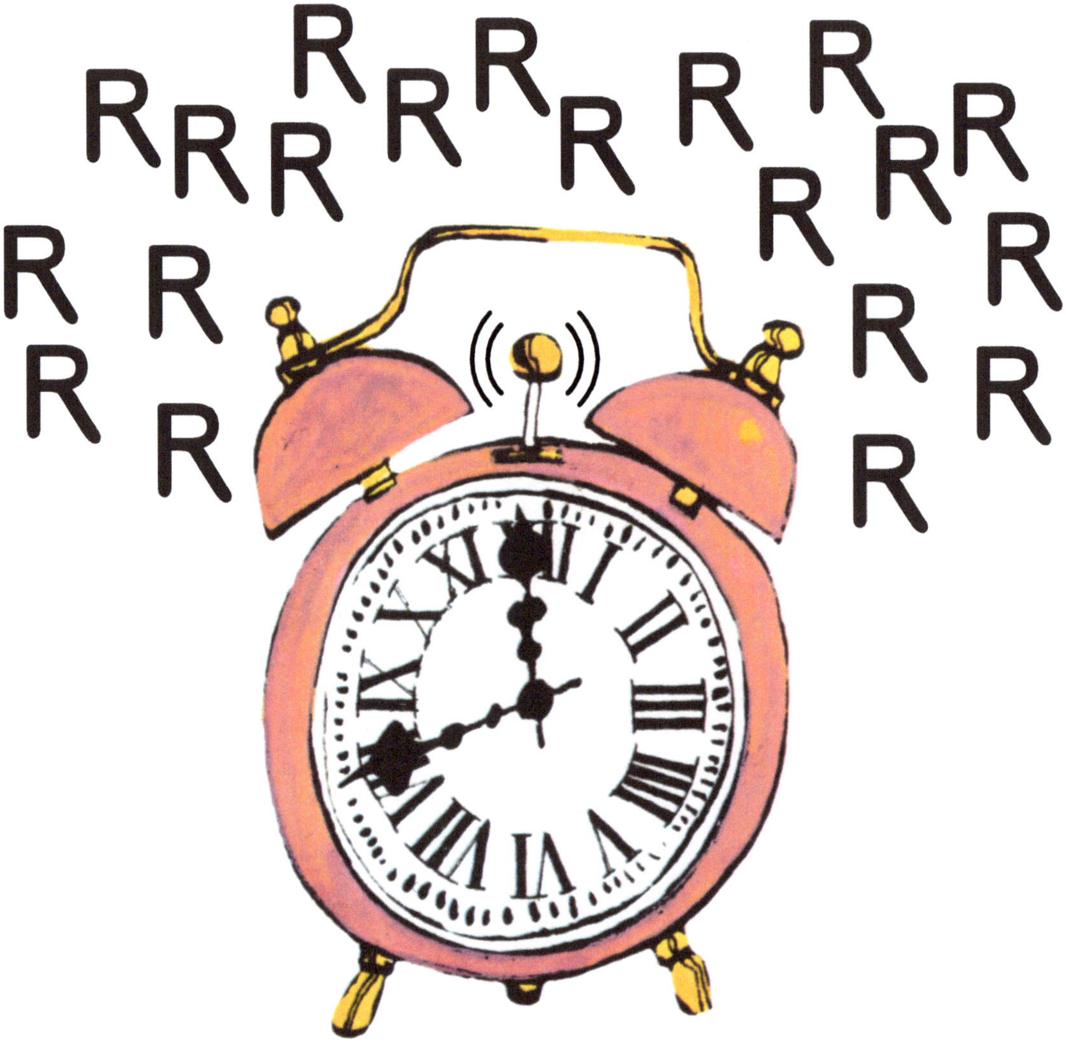
RRRRRRRRRRRRRRRRRRRR

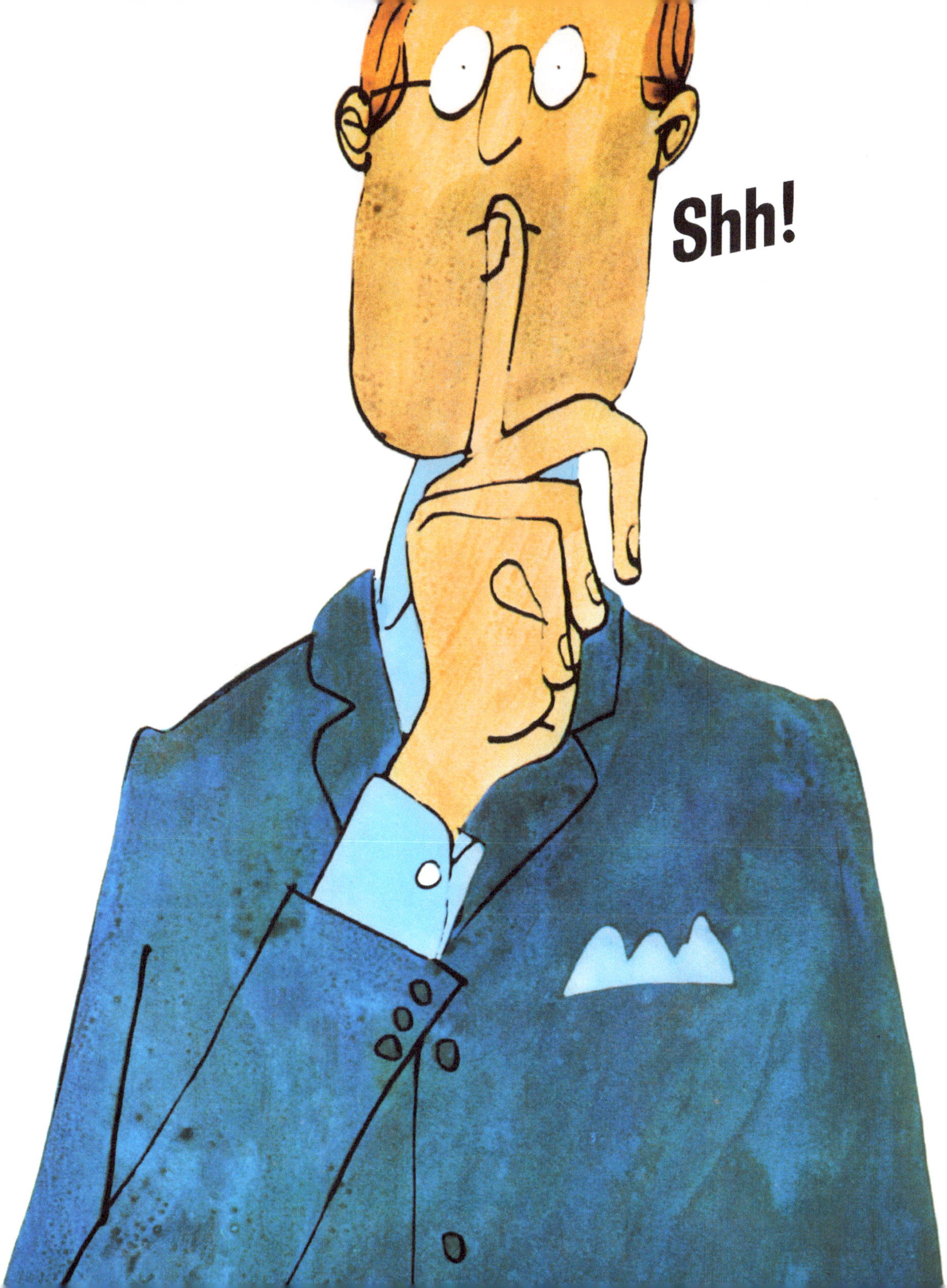
Shh!

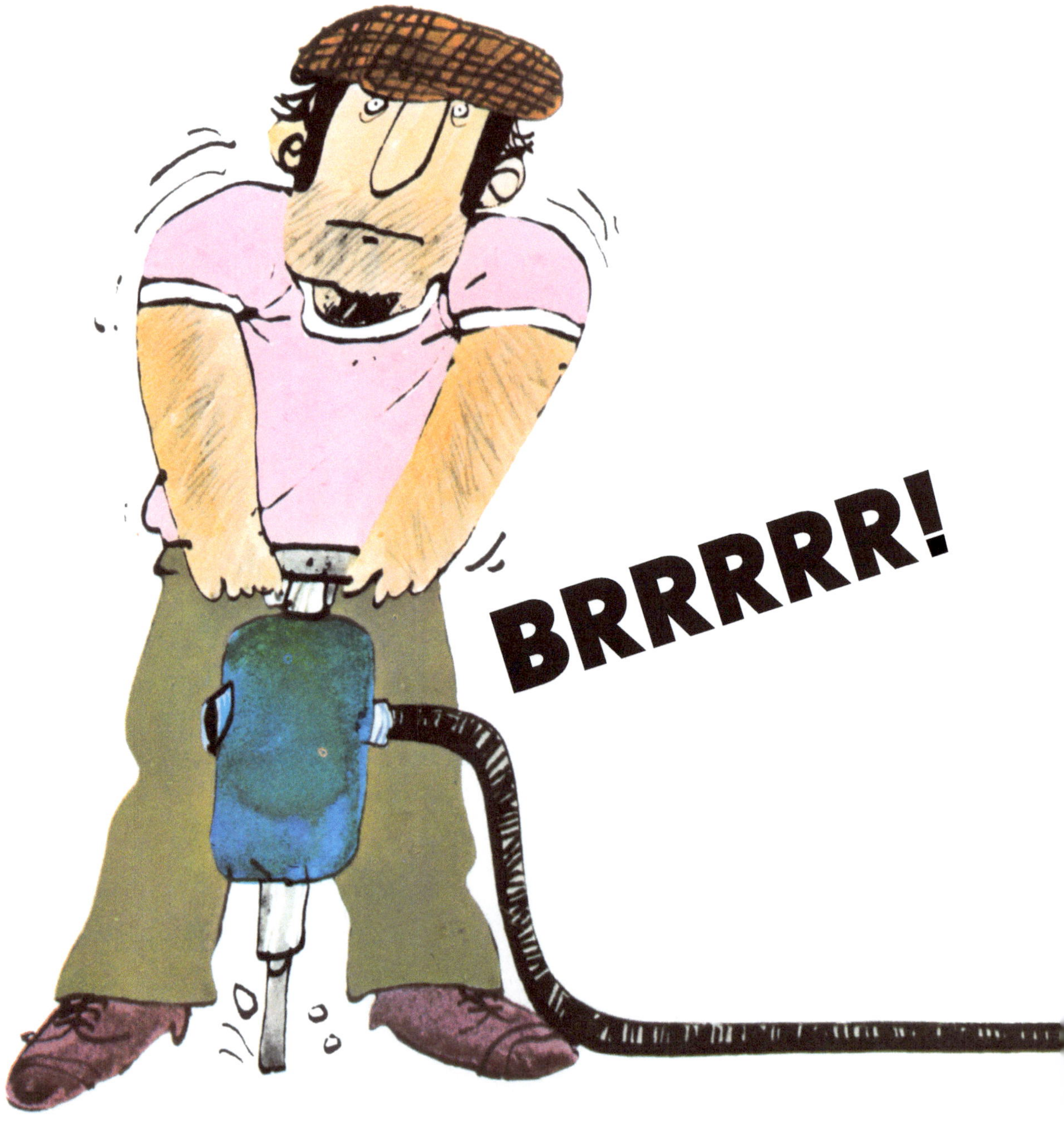
BRRRRR!

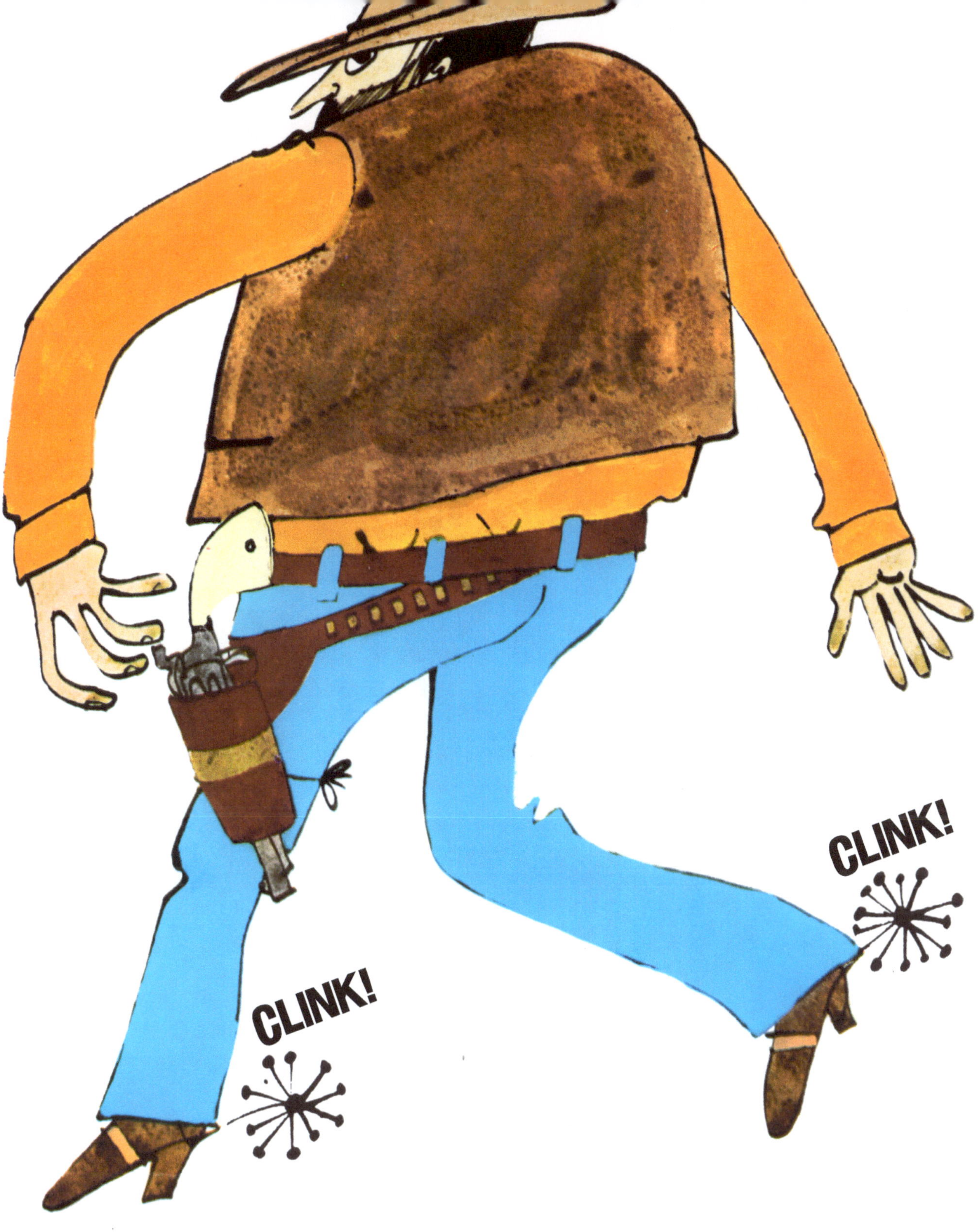
CLINK!
CLINK!

MOO!

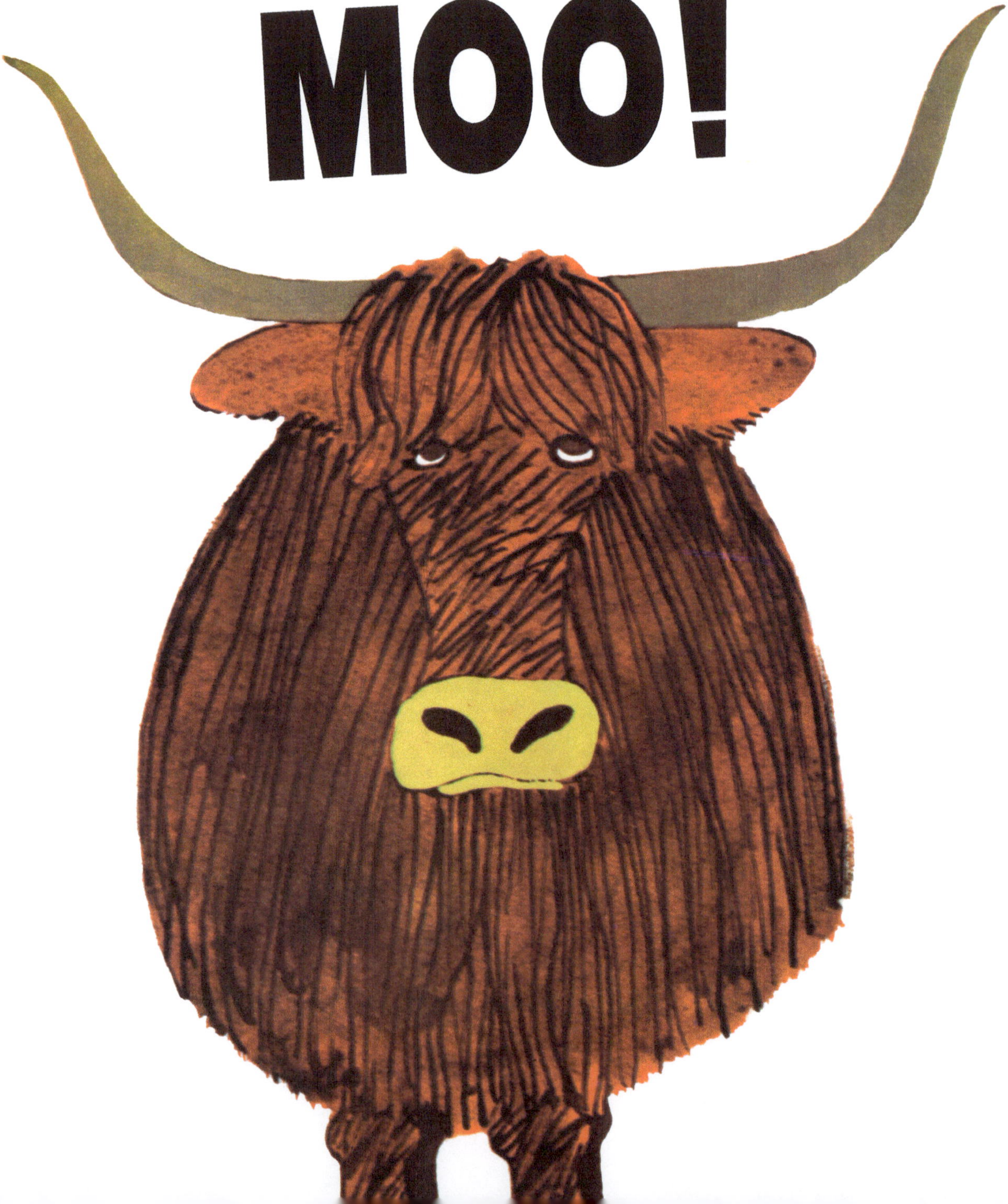

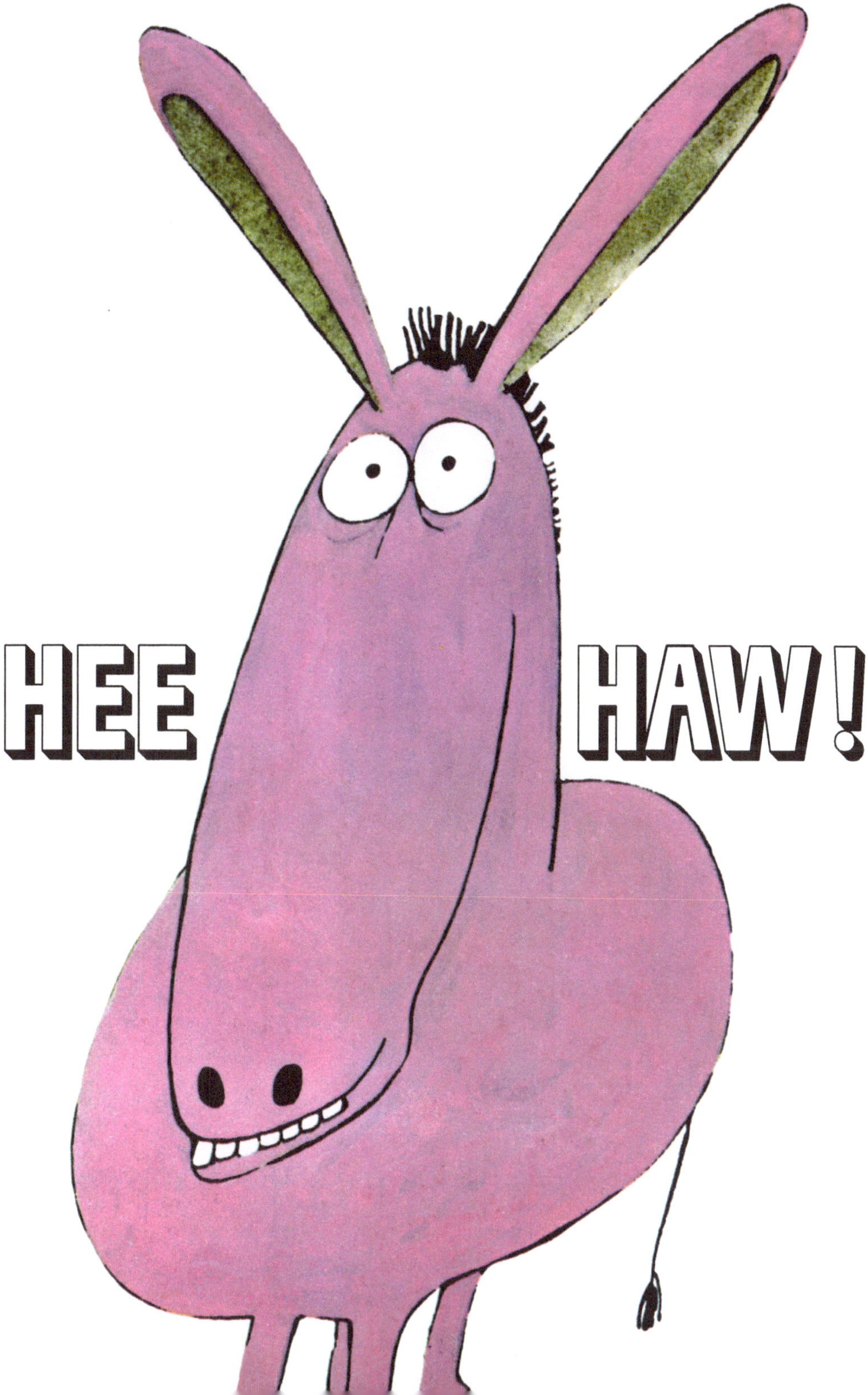
HEE HAW!

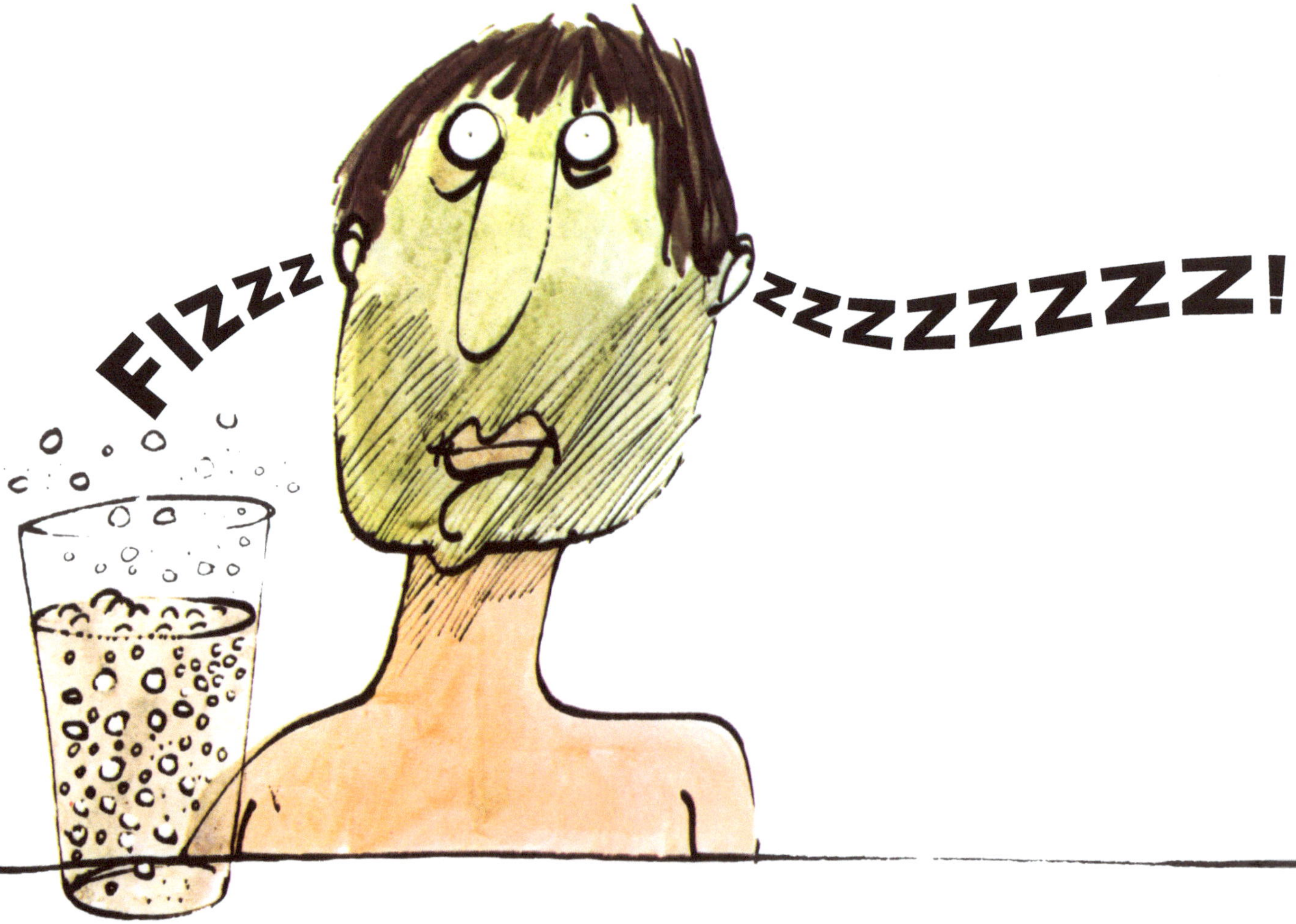
FIZZZ
ZZZZZZZZ!

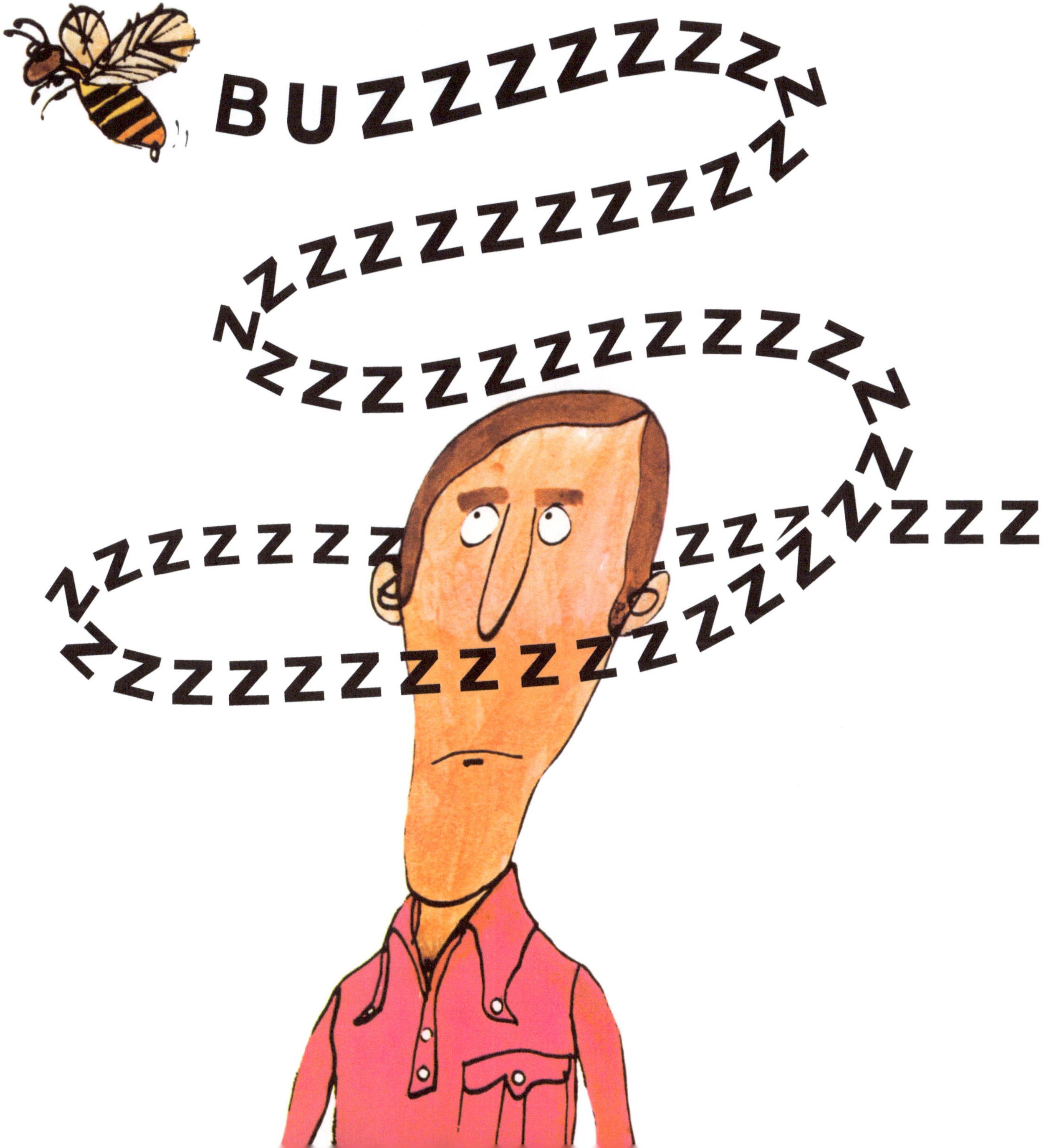
BUZZZZZZZZZZ

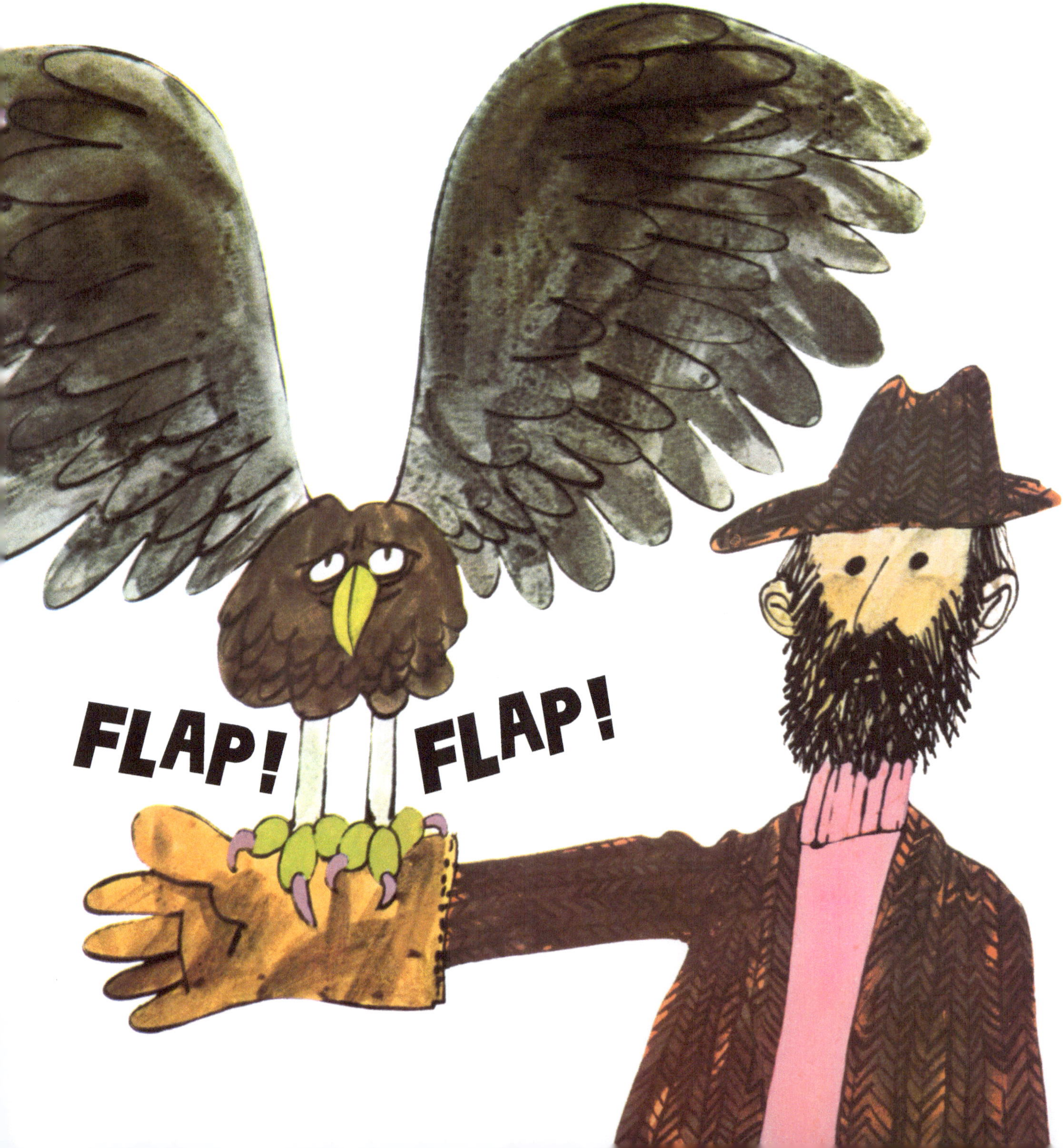
FLAP!
FLAP!

WOOF!
WOOF!

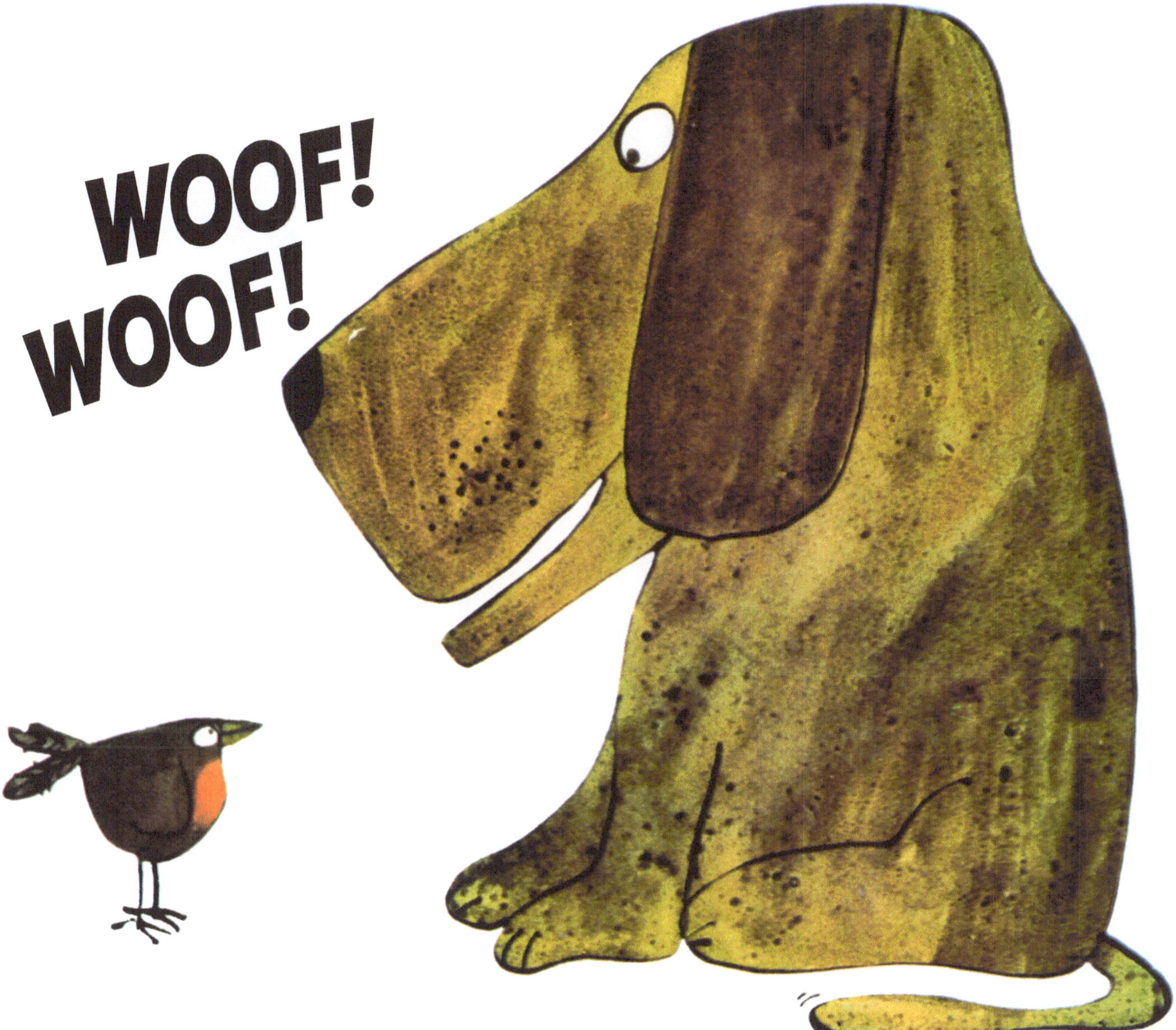

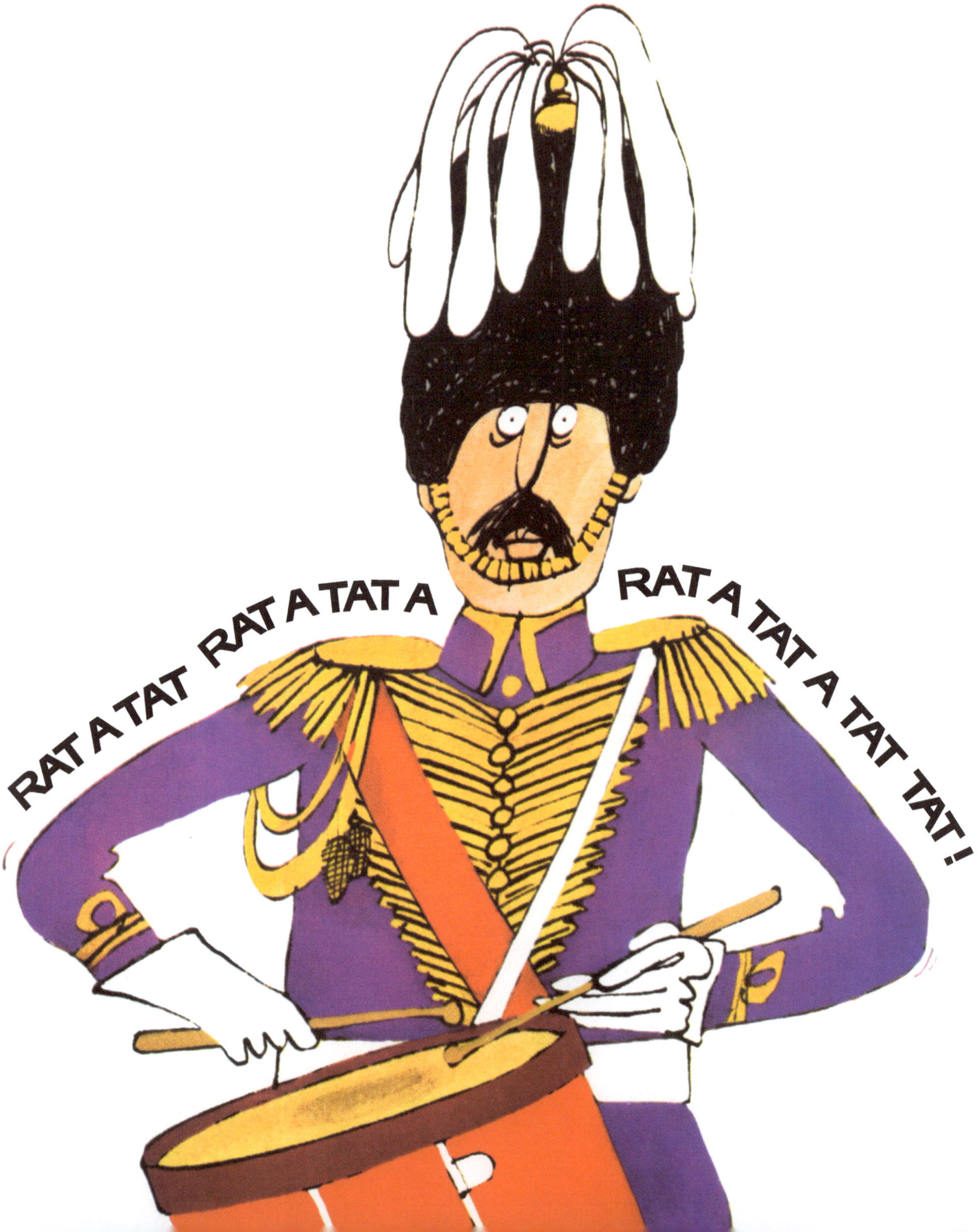
RAT A TAT RAT A TAT A RAT A TAT A TAT A TAT TAT TAT!

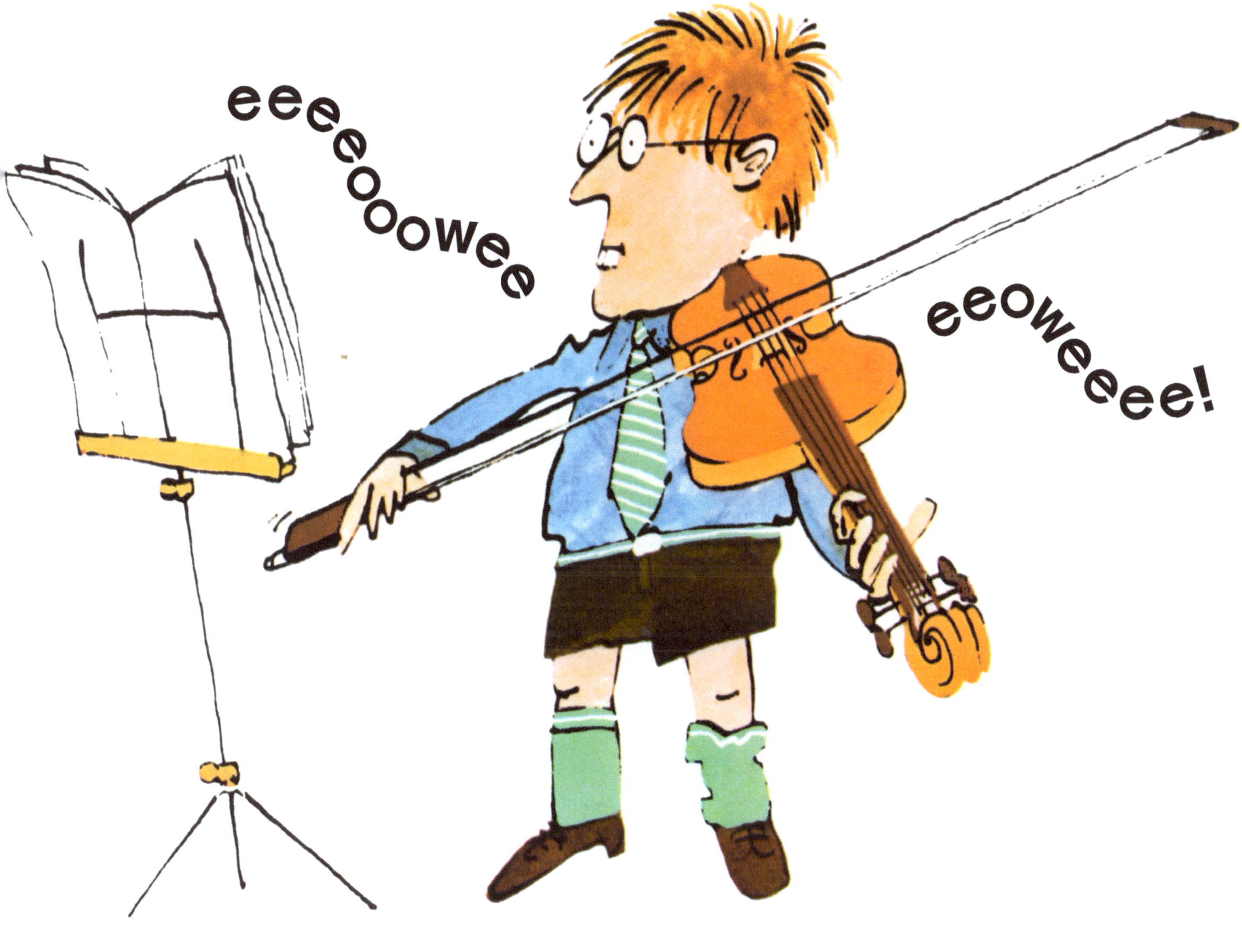
eeeeooowee
eeoweeee!

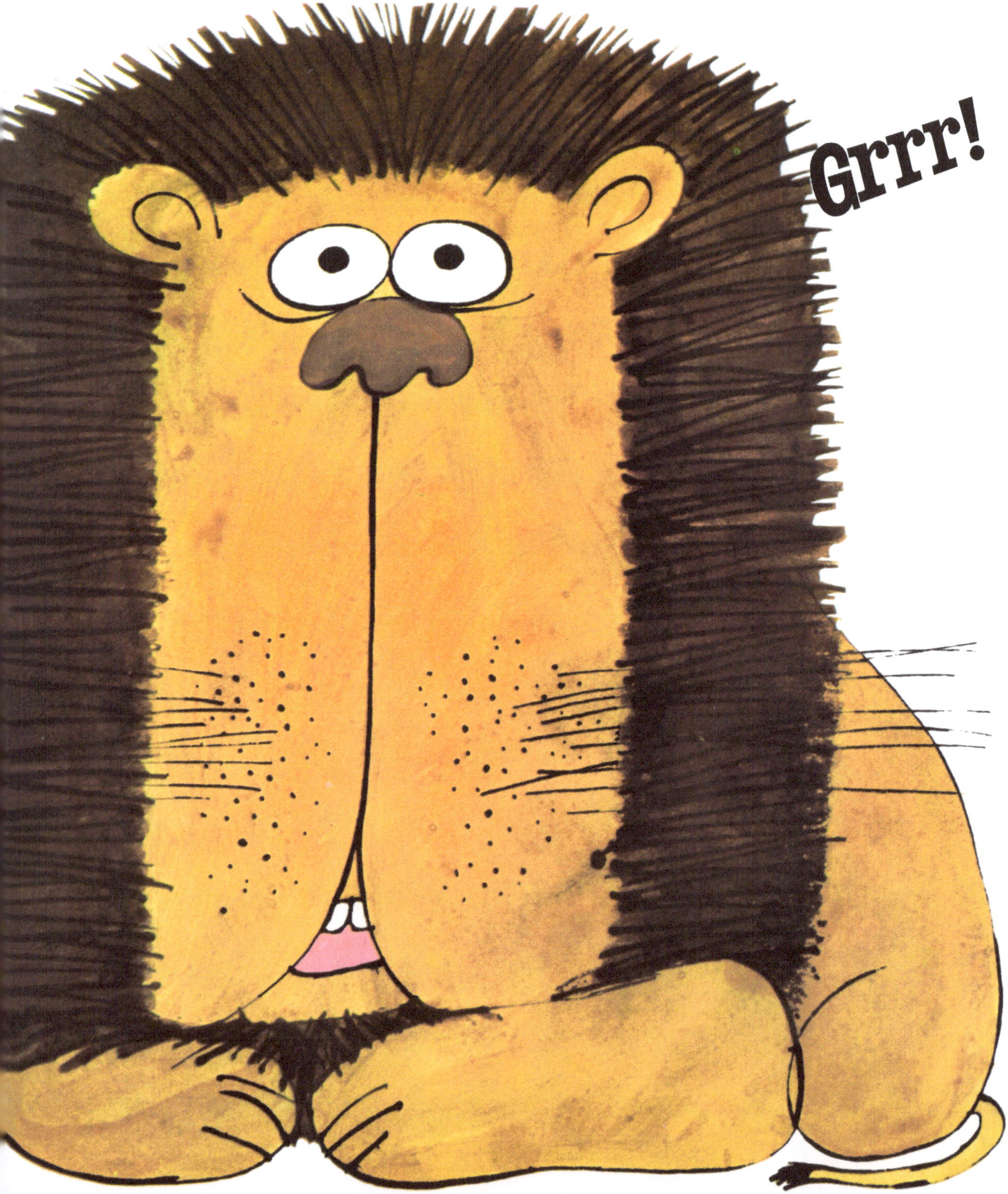
Grrr!

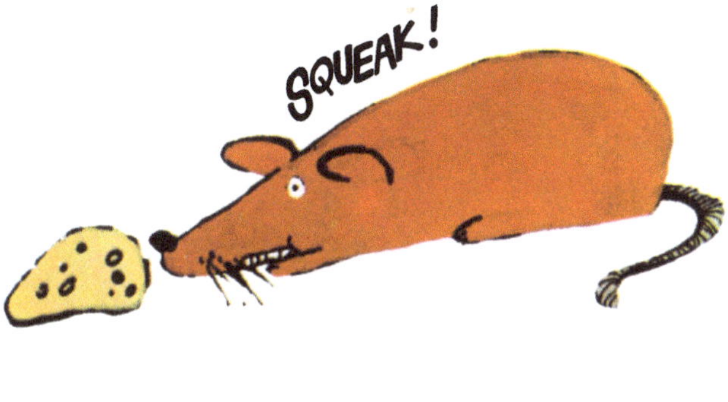
SQUEAK!

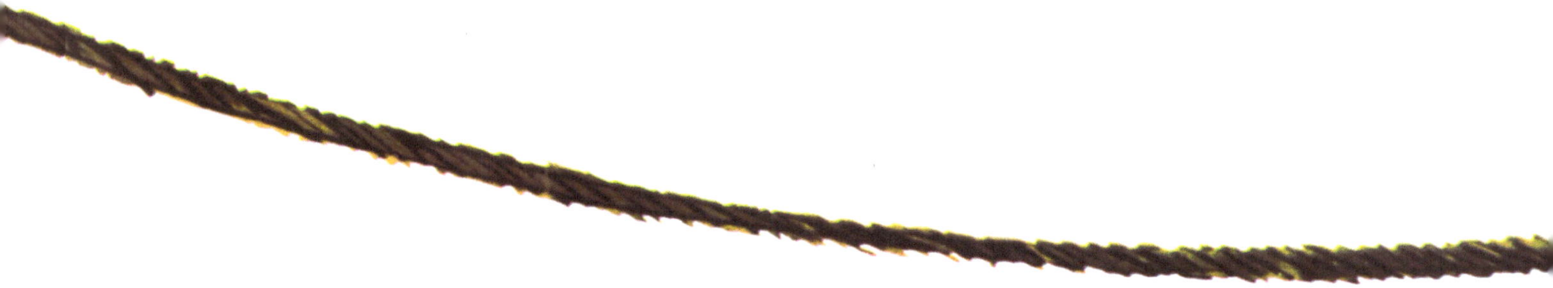

aaiiee

aa!

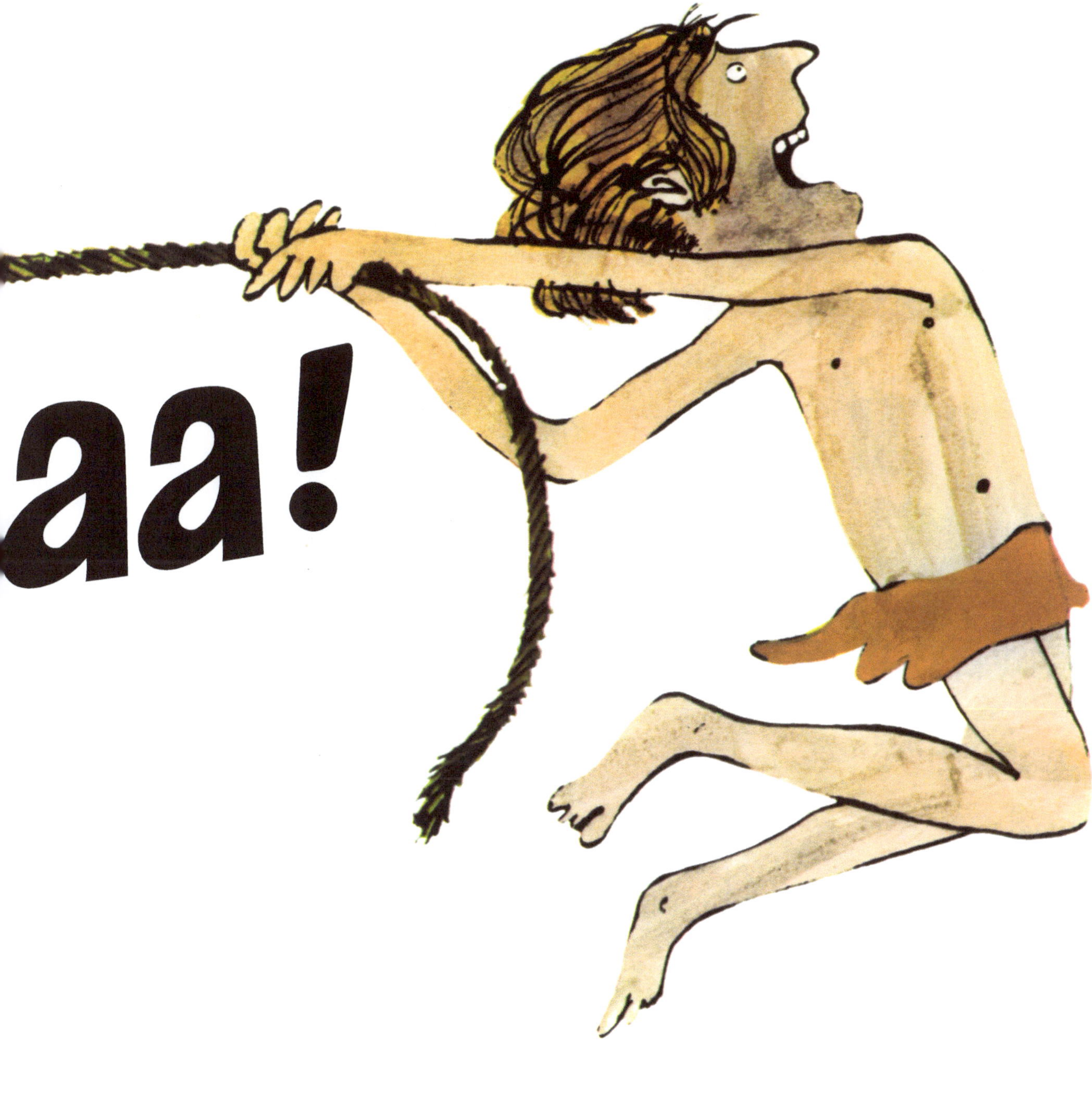

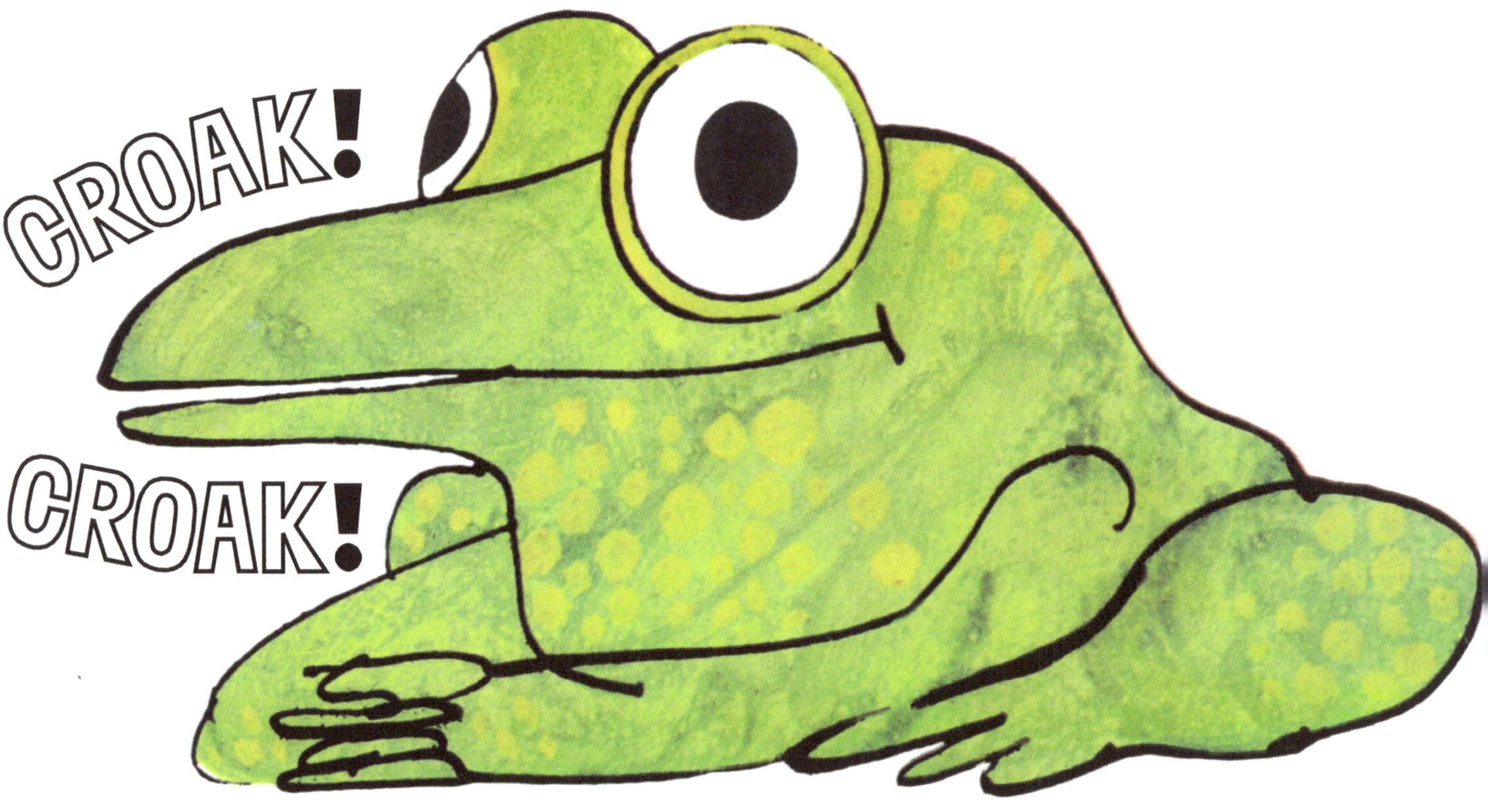
CROAK!
CROAK!

oink
oink!

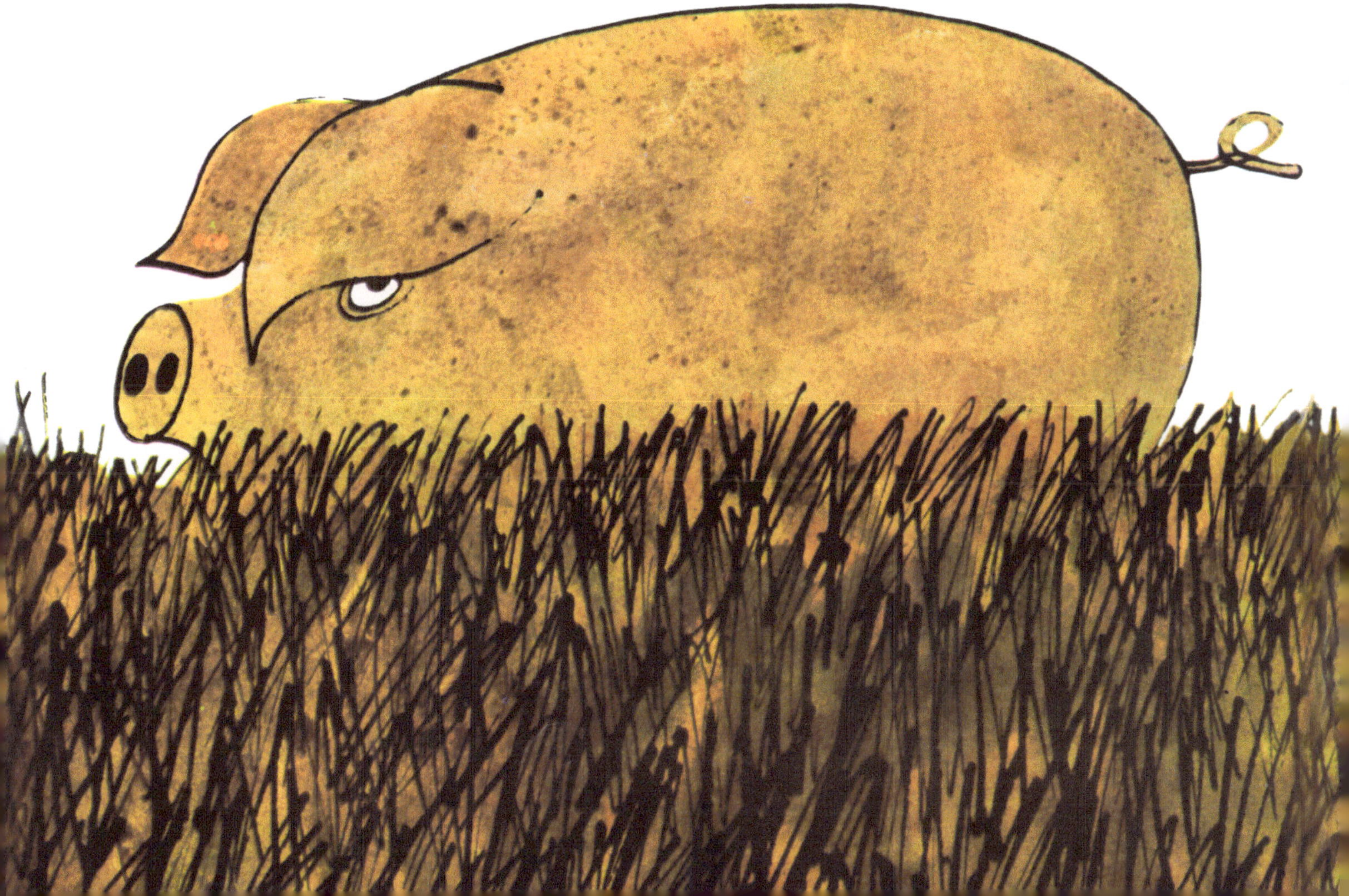

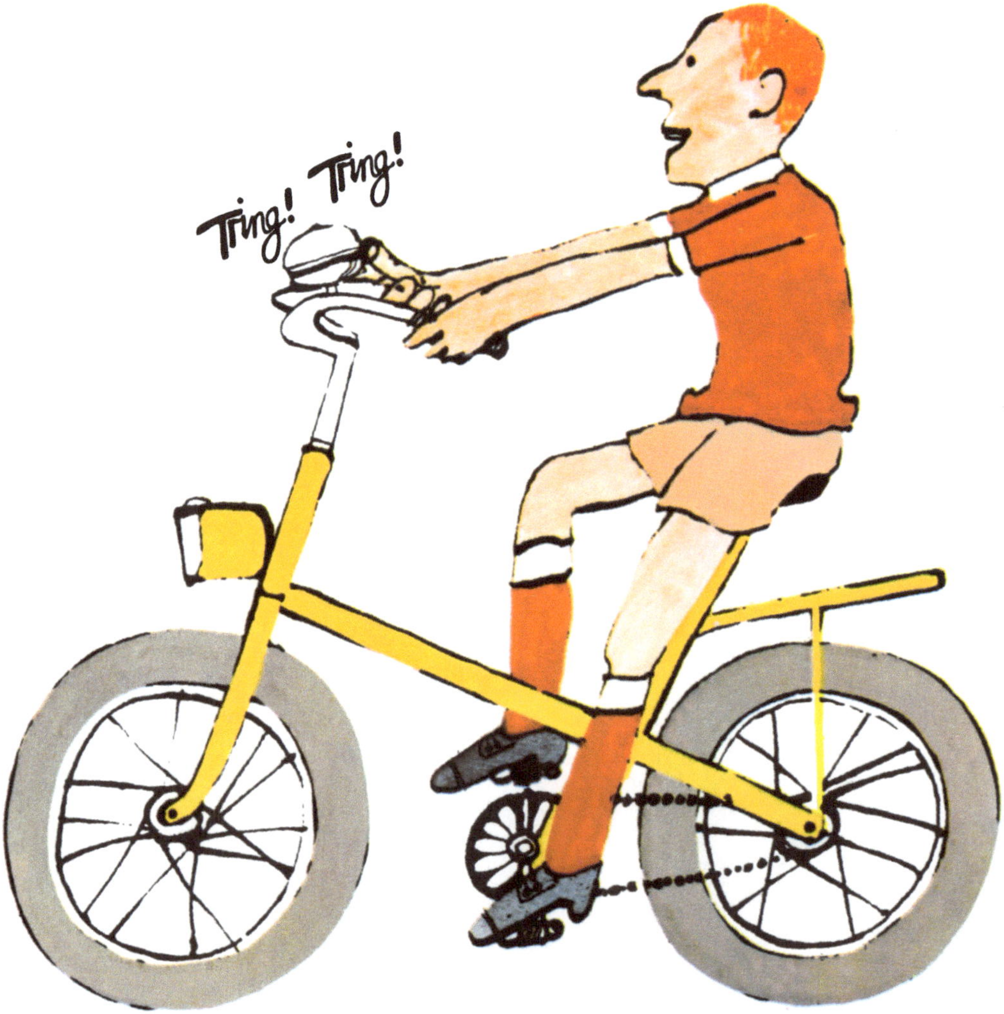
Tring! Tring!

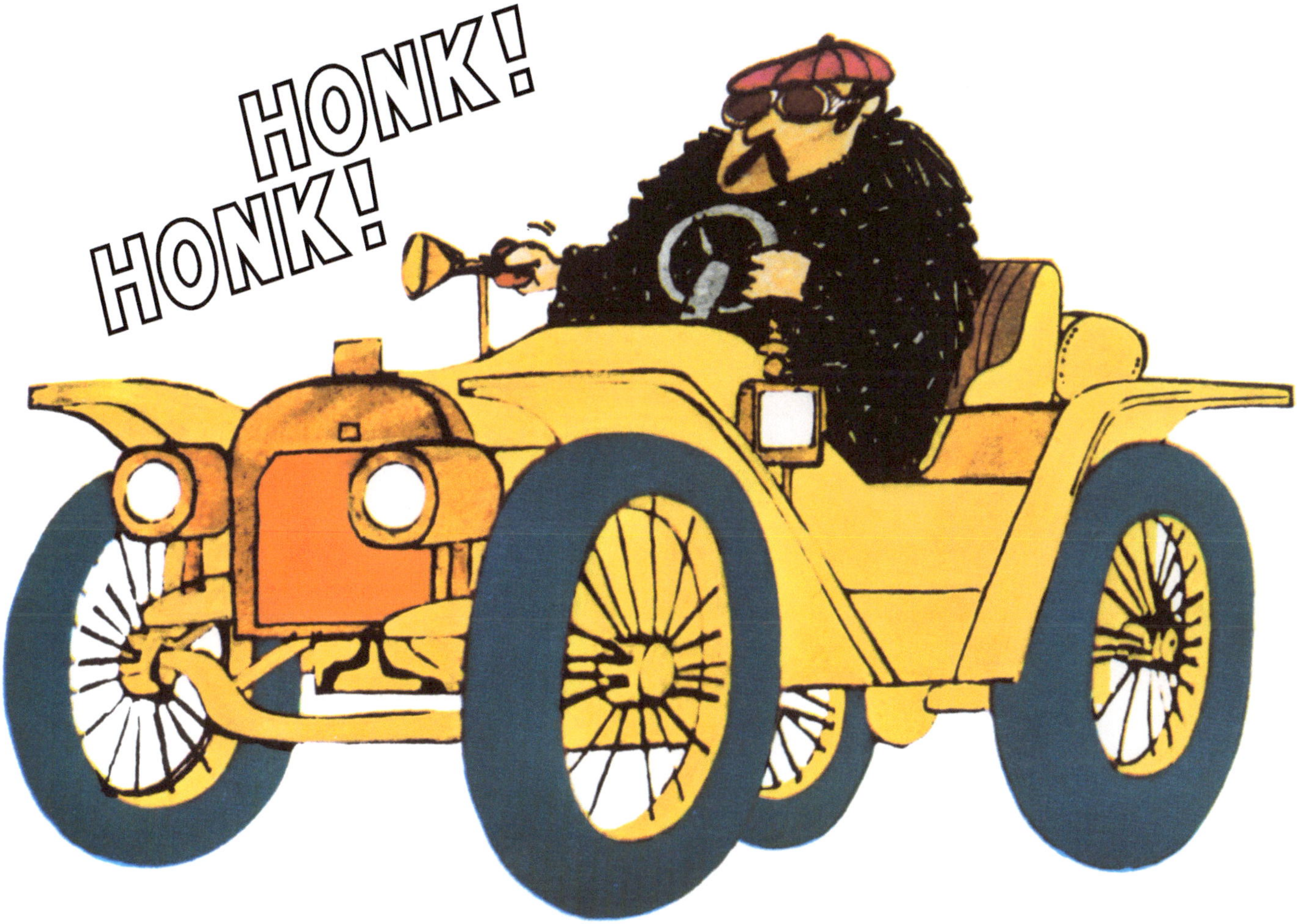
HONK!
HONK!

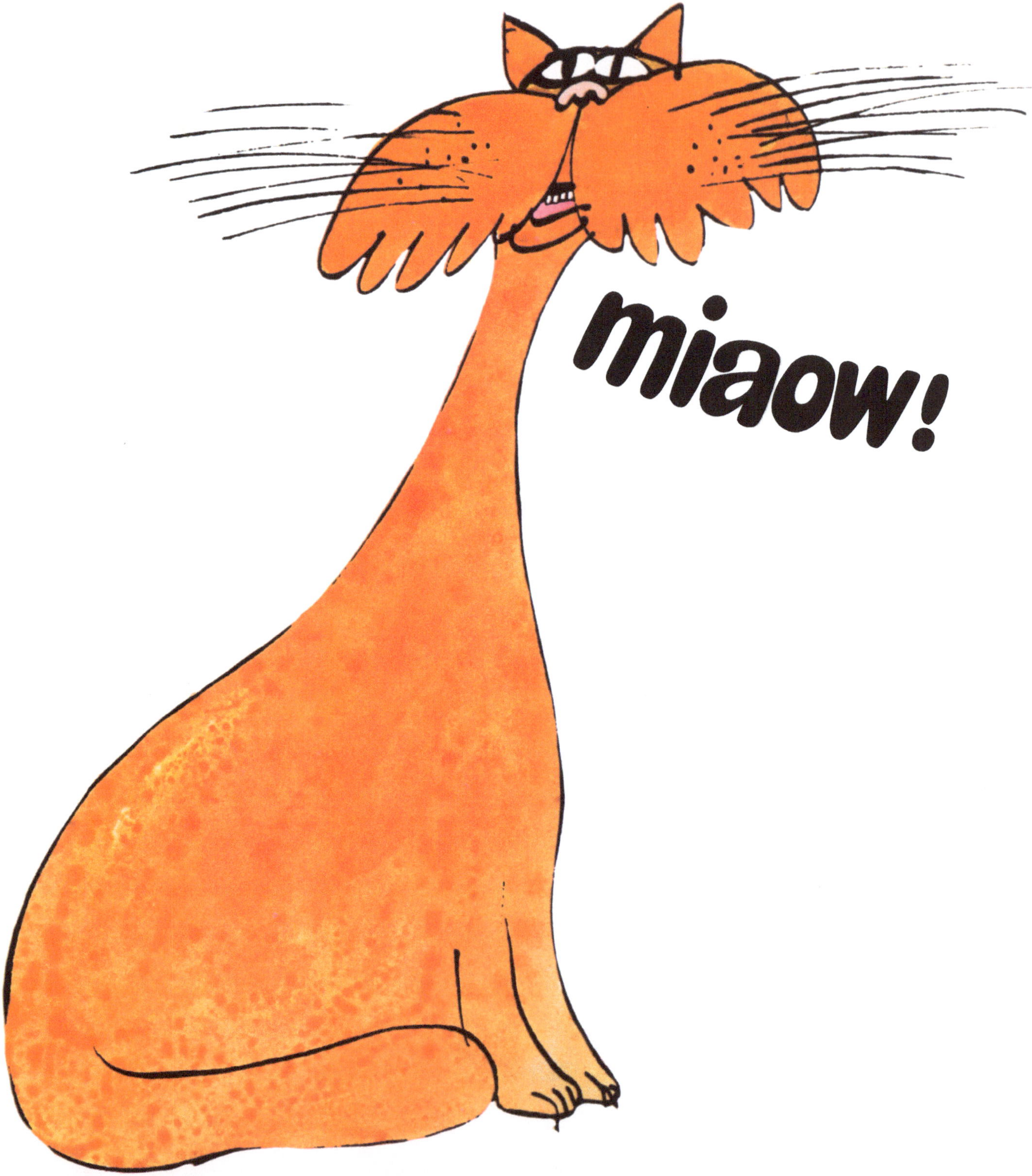
miaow!

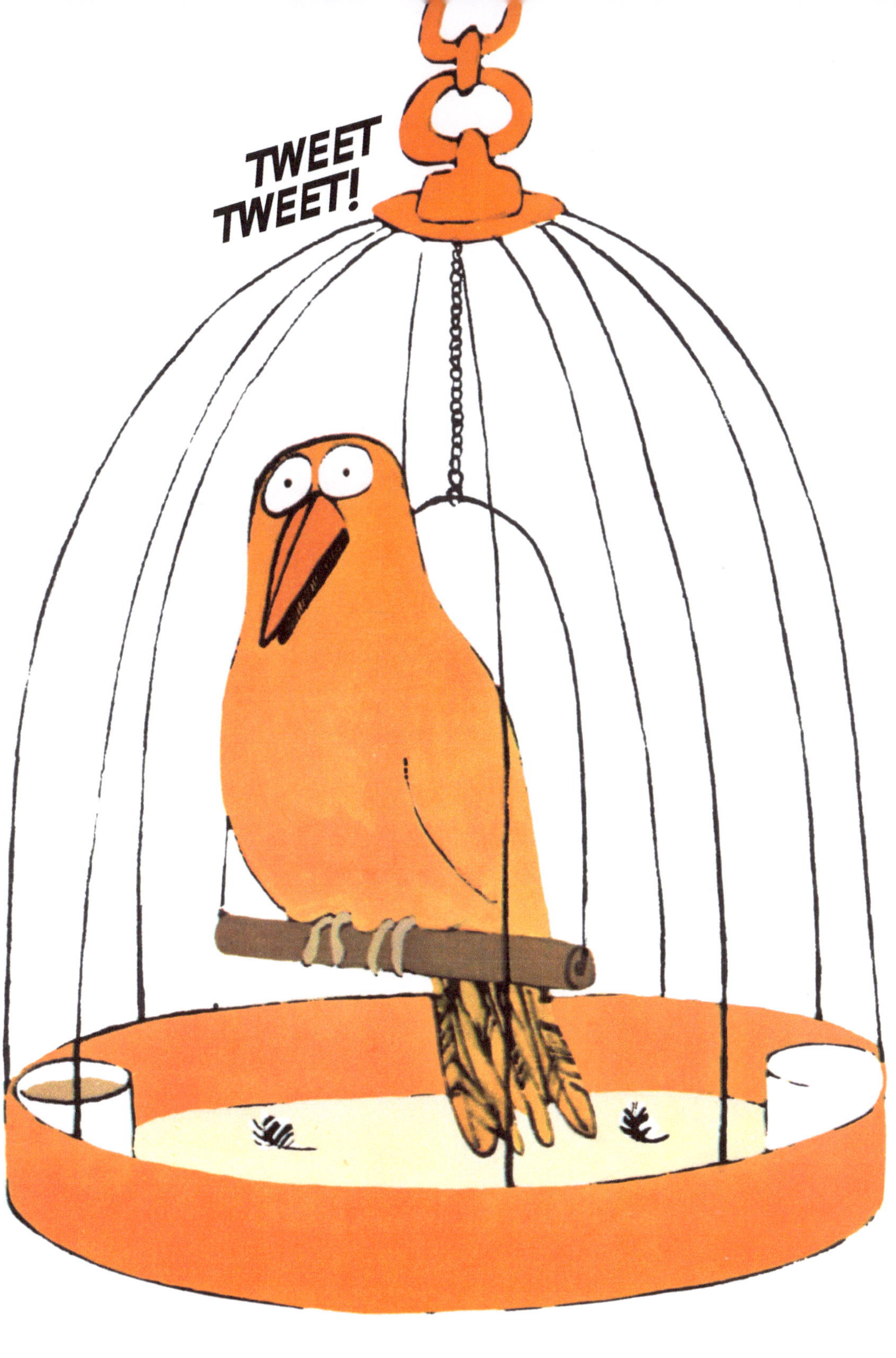
TWEET
TWEET!

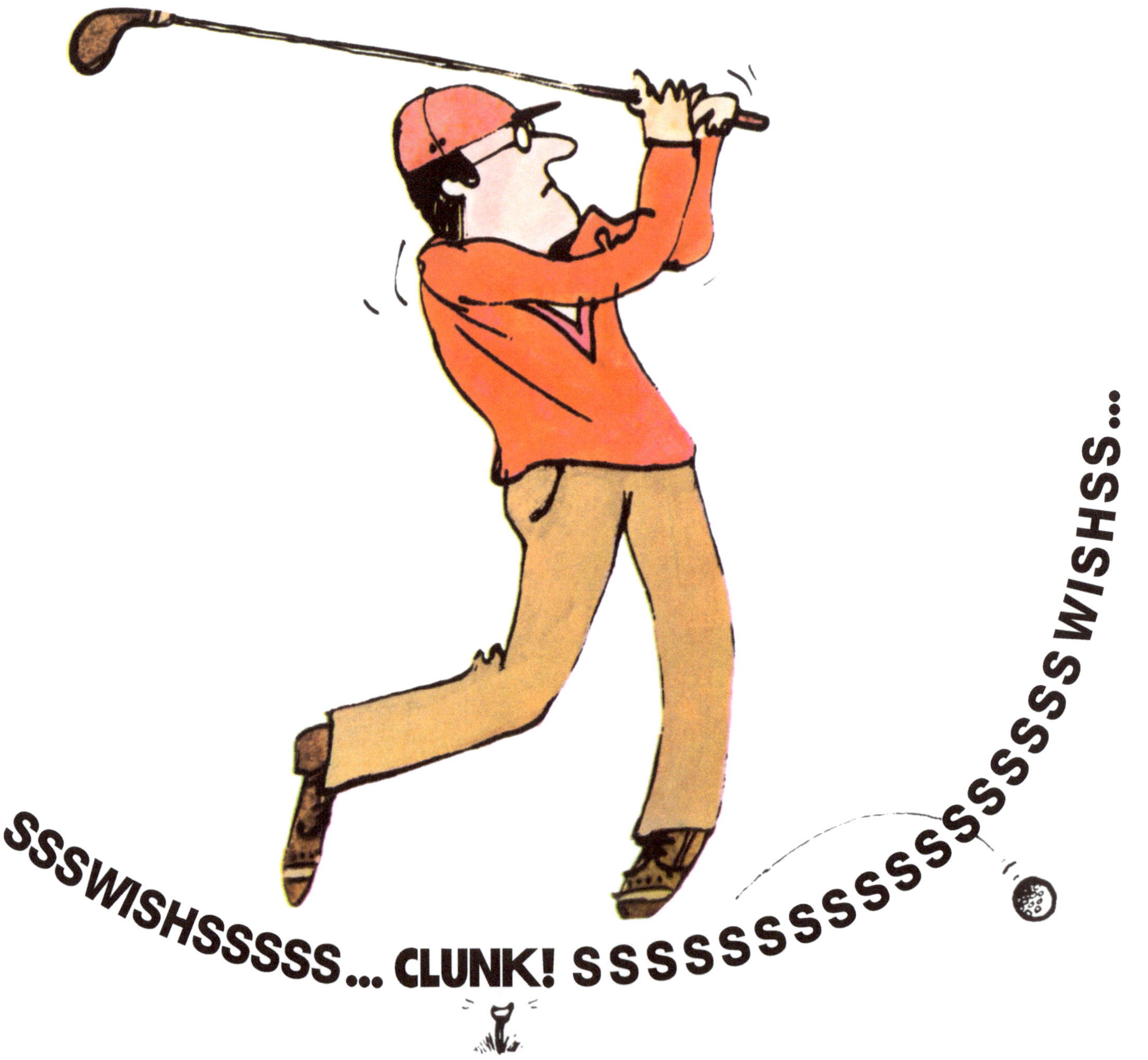
SSSWISHSSSSS... CLUNK! SSSSSSSSSSSSSSSSSSSSSWISHSS...

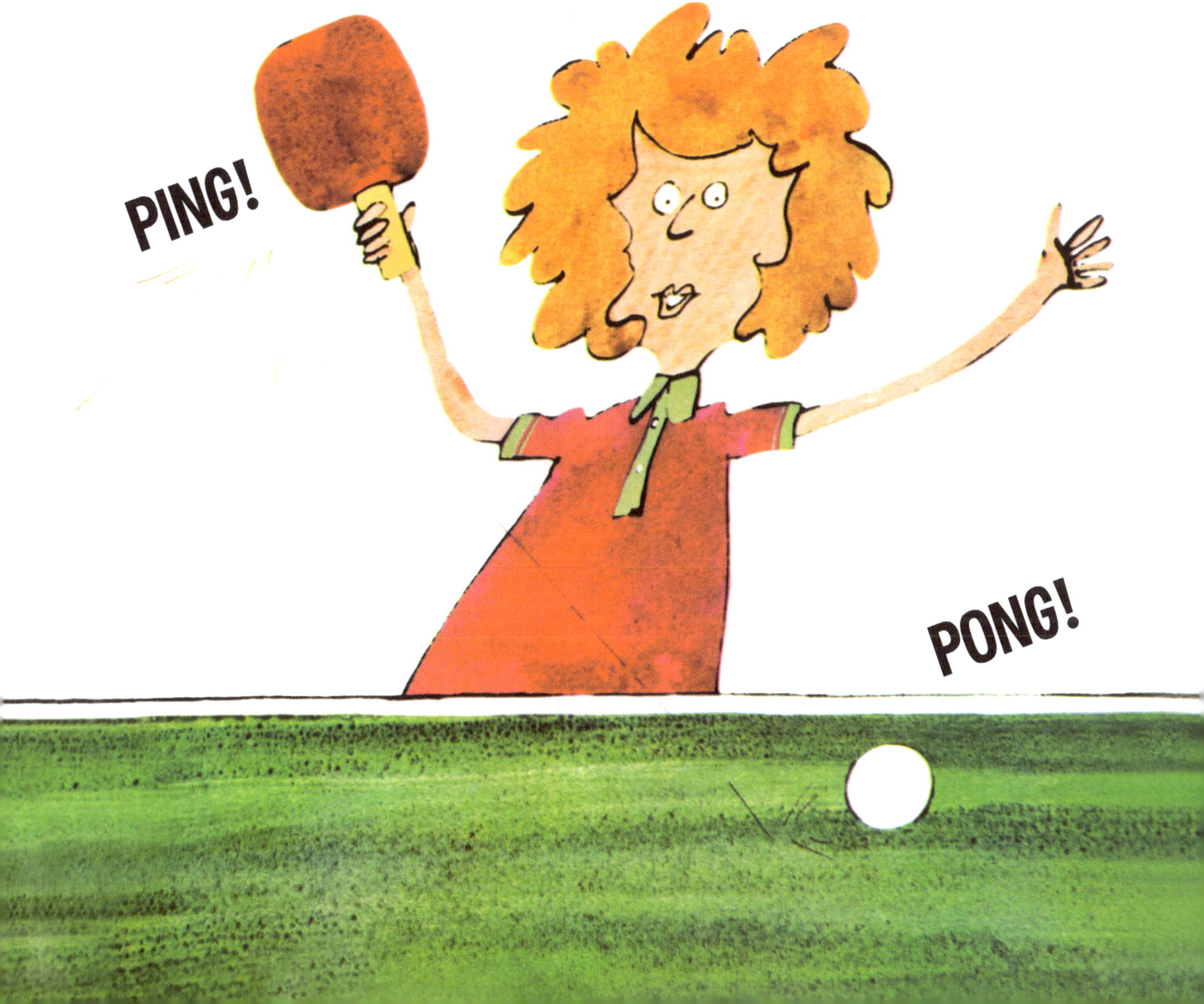
PING!
PONG!

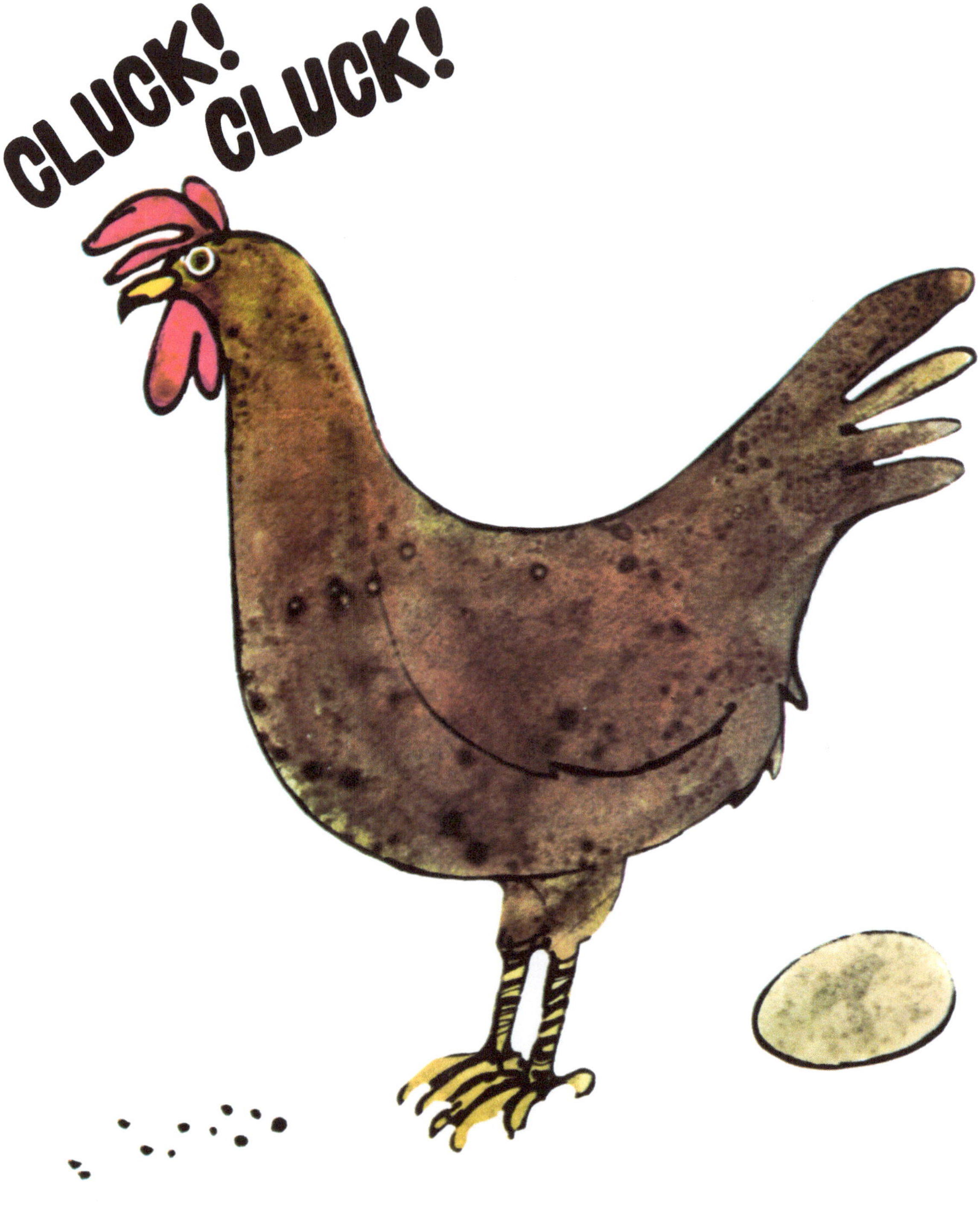
CLUCK! CLUCK!

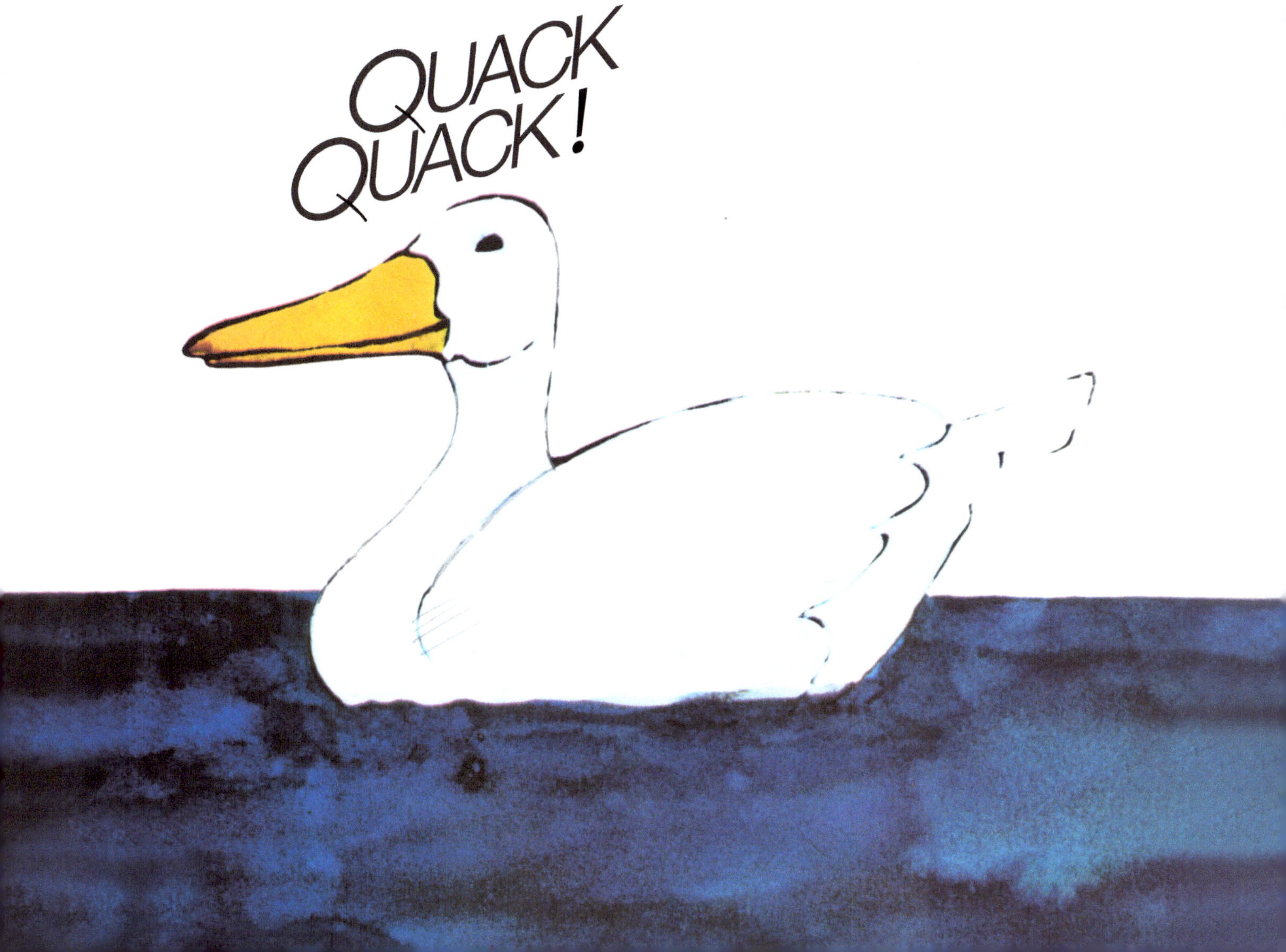
QUACK
QUACK!

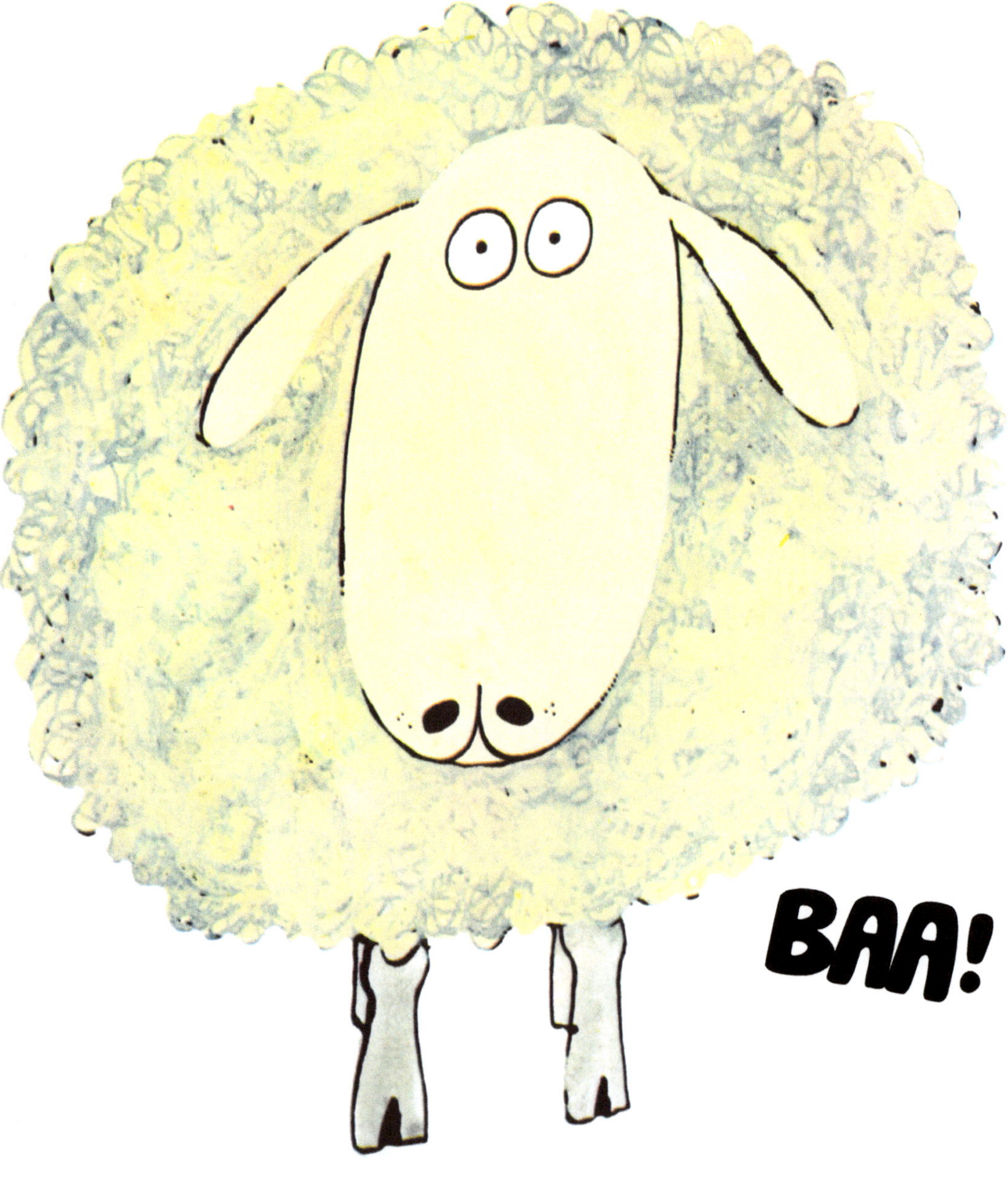

BAA!

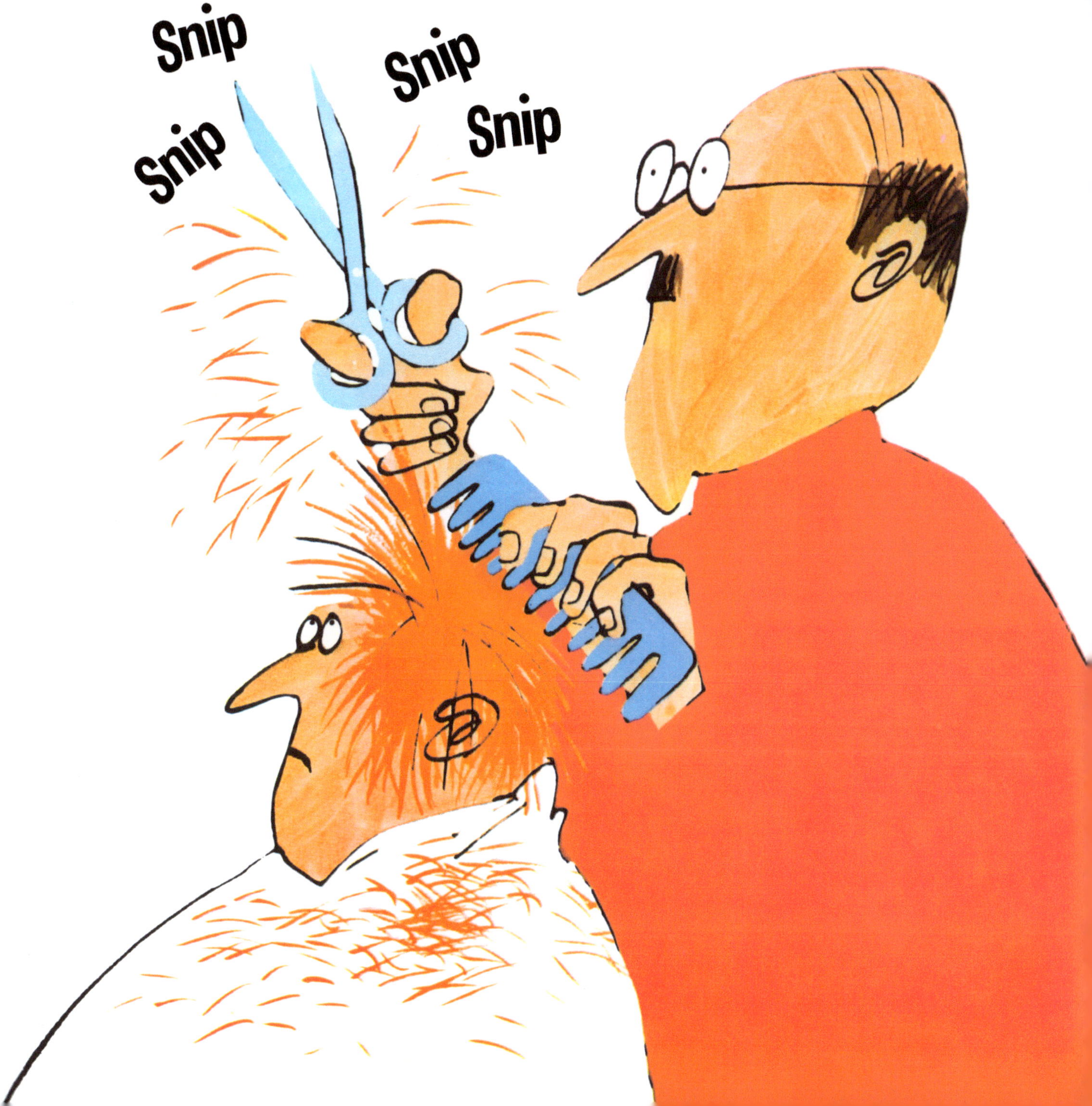
Snip
Snip
Snip
Snip

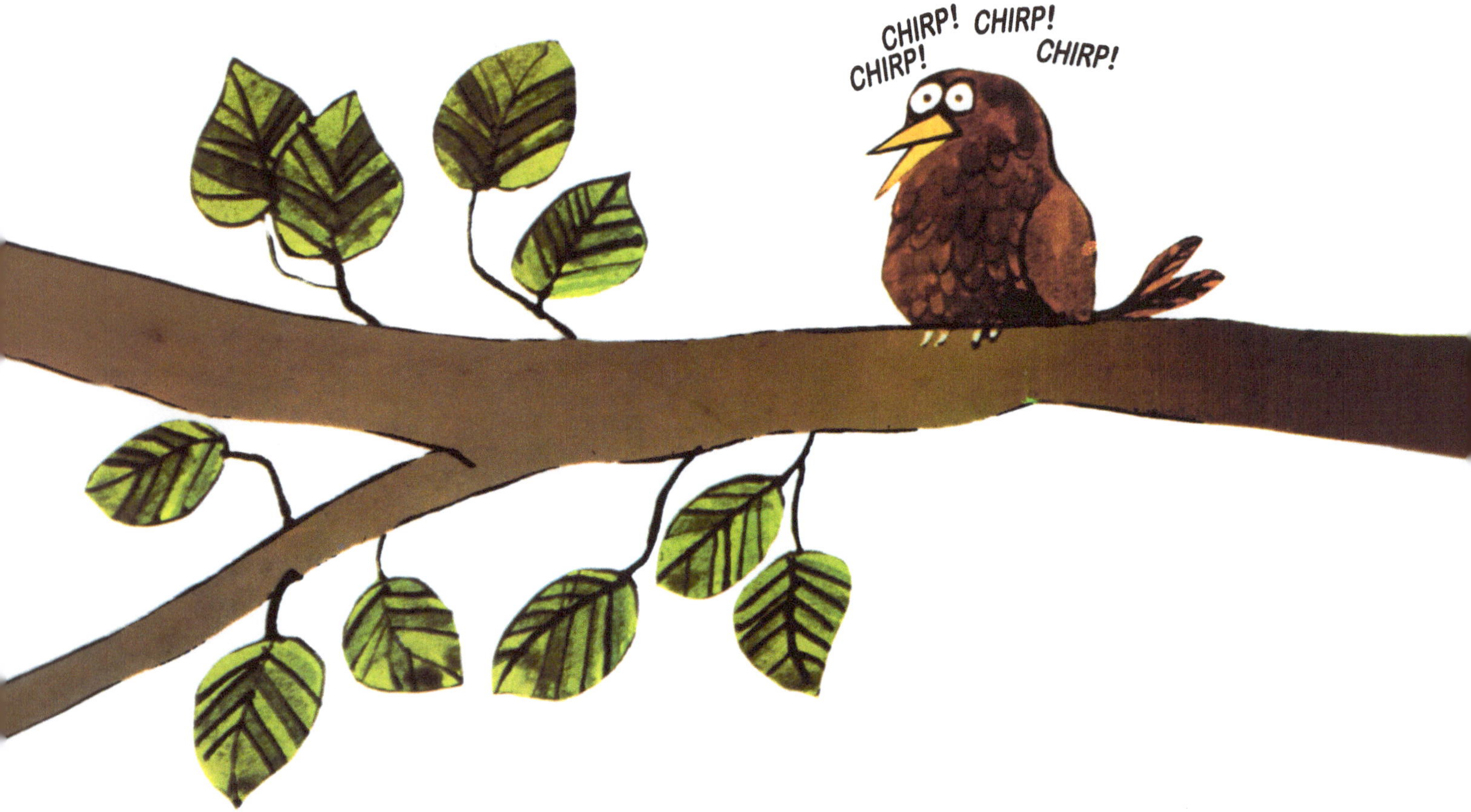
CHIRP!
CHIRP!
CHIRP!
CHIRP!

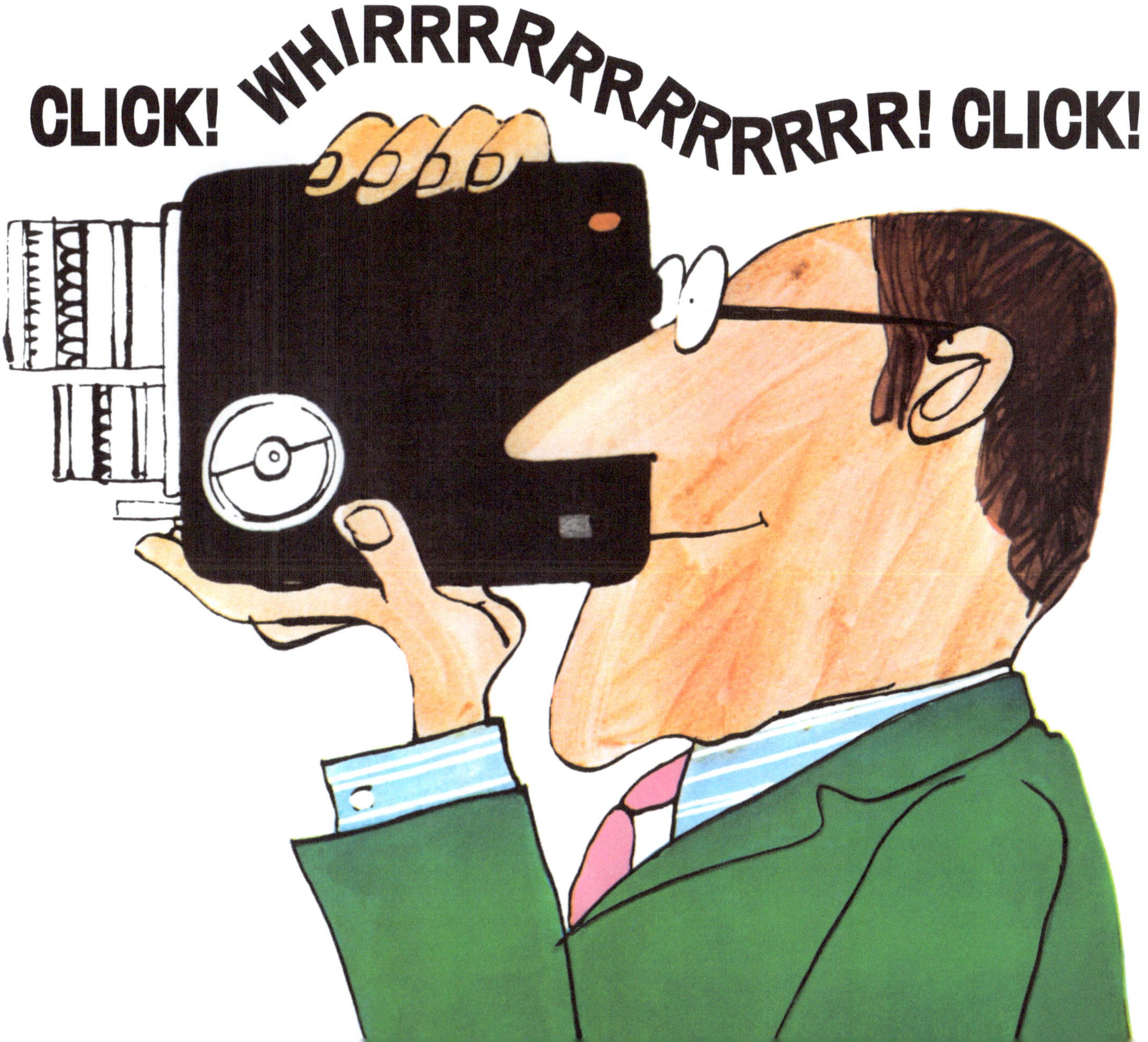
CLICK! WHIRRRRRRRRRRRR! CLICK!

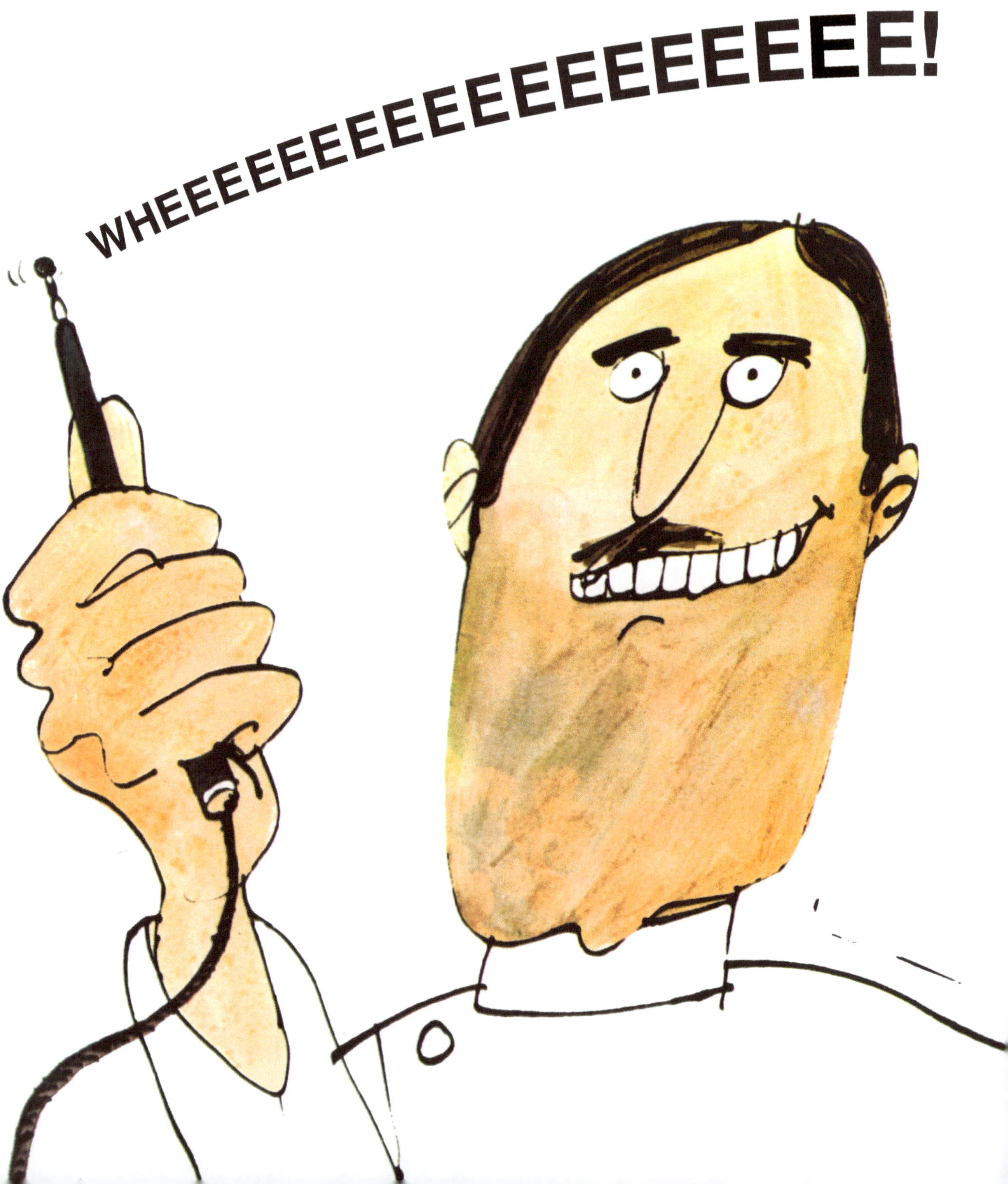
WHEEEEEEEEEEEEEEEEEE!

www.ingramcontent.com/pod-product-compliance
Lightning Source LLC
Chambersburg PA
CBHW051821210526
45473CB00005B/1688
* 9 7 9 8 7 3 9 0 3 6 5 3 7 *